A THEOLOGY OF
HOLINESS

HISTORICAL, EXEGETICAL, AND PHILOSOPHICAL PERSPECTIVES

ALEC GOLDSTEIN

KODESH PRESS

A Theology of Holiness:
Historical, Exegetical, and Philosophical Perspectives

© Alec Goldstein, 2018

ISBN: 978-1-947857-10-0

Paperback Edition

About the Cover

Jerusalem in Her Grandeur (1860)
Henry Courtney Selous

Published & Distributed Exclusively by

Kodesh Press L.L.C.
New York, NY
www.kodeshpress.com
kodeshpress@gmail.com

CONTENTS

Preface

The idea of holiness is central to religious behavior. Most if not all religions have a notion of there being something "holy," with special rules, privileges, and restrictions, associated with that holiness. I have undertaken to, however imperfectly, study that concept from a primarily biblical and Jewish perspective.

There are three proximate causes of this book. First is a public speaking class I took at Yeshiva University in New York. Aspiring rabbinical students would deliver practice sermons each week, invariably based on the weekly Torah reading. One week was *Parashat Ḳedoshim* (Lev. 19:1-20:27), which opens with the words, "And the Lord spoke to Moses saying: Speak to the entire assembly of Israel and say to them: Be holy, because I the Lord your God am holy" (Lev. 19:2). What followed, based on this verse, were three very erudite, persuasive, and systematic explanations of what holiness means in Judaism. And yet they all were contradictory. It seemed peculiar to me that a concept of this magnitude was subject to such variety of interpretation.

Second was that for a while I had taken an interest in logical positivism and then analytic philosophy. Logical positivism as a movement has long been shifted to the philosophical scrapheap, but it has added two critical questions to my repertoire: "What does that mean?" and "How do you know it?" In other words, when a statement about metaphysics (i.e., something that does not exist in the physical sense) is made, what is that statement reducible to? Is it an irreducible *sui generis* concept, does it have component parts, and if so what are they? I found that when dealing with grand abstract ideas like goodness, justice, or mercy, asking myself these questions was a useful and clarifying exercise. The other question was also crucial: "How do I know it?" What standard of evidence, of proof, could be used for metaphysical propositions that seem to have no correspondence in the physical world? The standard of proof for metaphysical propositions must be much lower than the standard of proof for propositions about the physical universe, and that also means that the level of certainty often needs to be adjusted downward. Applying this to holiness, I was able to find that some people applied holiness to various forms of separation, while others ascribed it to a certain sensation or feeling, while still others said holiness was a *sui generis* and irreducible concept. But what was their evidence? Looking back, I have referred to this as "textual epistemology." By this term I mean that if a person puts forward a theory then I would ask for the scriptural source. One person said that her theory of holiness is that when you go grocery shopping and realize you don't want an item in your cart, you put it back in the right place. I told her that I think that's a wonderful thing to do, but asked her how that related to the biblical idea of holiness.

If philosophers from Aristotle to Kant to Van Inwagen say that statements about the physical universe can be measured by means of comparison to the physical world, then by "textual epistemology," I mean that statements about belief can be measured by means of comparison to the sacred text. Obviously, the Bible, the Talmud, and the vast corpus of early rabbinic and Medieval literature is open to interpretation, but it at least gives a starting point for a discussion.

The third proximate cause of this work is a class I took with Dr. Richard Steiner called "Hebrew Semantics and Lexicography." Dr. Steiner is one of the greatest scholars on Hebrew and Semitic languages, and a *mentsch* in the truest sense of the word. He allowed me to remain in that class even though my background was not as strong as that of my peers, but I benefitted tremendously from it nonetheless. For the final assignment, we were required to take two Hebrew words with overlapping meanings and compare them. I decided that I wanted to finally write my paper on holiness and get it done with (this was back in 2011!), so I proposed researching the semantic overlap between the roots *k-d-sh*, "holy," and *t-h-r*, "pure." Yet I became fixated on every aspect of this relationship: linguistic (the focus of the class), anthropological, exegetical, literary, and philosophical. I had so much research, and was writing and rewriting so much that I blew past the due date and got an incomplete in the course.

My apologies, Dr. Steiner, for never handing in that final paper. The present study does not meet the original parameters in scope or length, but I want you to know that were it not for your class and for your most useful guidance along the way, this current project would not have been completed.

*

Perhaps like many works when they are done, one wonders if the work is a curiosity or a worthwhile contribution. That will be for the readers to decide. My approach, besides for the "textual epistemology" referenced above, is to trace the idea of holiness and the Semitic root *k-d-sh* from pre-biblical times forward. To do this, I have been forced to rely on the works of many scholars who do not share my beliefs about revelation, the divinity of the Bible, or the authority of the Rabbis. This reliance is an obvious deficiency in the present work, because my interest is how holiness has been understood in Jewish philosophy from a traditional perspective. However, I see value in studying how the word "holy" is used in pre-biblical Semitic languages like Ugaritic and Akkadian. On the one hand, when one observes the linguistic similarities between Biblical Hebrew and surrounding languages, it is hard to refute that the Bible did not emerge—at least to some extent—from the culture that enveloped it. On the other hand, the Hebrew Bible is not merely another ancient Near Eastern text, and it is tragic how cavalierly it is treated in certain academic circles.

I have placed heavy emphasis on the biblical text itself, along with the masters of our tradition, the principal commentaries that are the building blocks of the Jewish faith. Earlier versions of this work merely compared different Medieval interpretations of the idea of holiness—specifically the interpretations put forward by Rashi, Maimonides, and Nahmanides. However, every comment of theirs forced me to work backwards to scrutinize their support, until the focus was shifted largely to the biblical era. My primary objective was to write a book of Jewish philosophy based on classical

Jewish sources from a traditional perspective. In the final form, the reader has to wait until the last few chapters until I felt that sufficient groundwork was laid to responsibly present the Medieval and modern material.

*

In the decade or so that I have been researching for this project, I have spoken to so many people that it is impossible to thank them all. Some are worthy of specific mention. First is Rabbi Chaim Bronstein, the Administrator of Rabbi Isaac Elchanan Theological Seminary of Yeshiva University. Rabbi Bronstein rides the A train from Bayswater, Queens, to Washington Heights every day, and he read an earlier version of this work during his commute, which is an hour and a half each way. Rabbi Yeshayahu Ginsburg also read through this work and offered much constructive insight. And Rabbi Ari Kahn was extremely generous with his time in reading the entire manuscript, for which I am indebted. Thank you also to Mitchell First, who generously agreed to proofread this work, and made many corrections.

Thank you also to Mr. Zvi Erenyi and Rabbi Moshe Schapiro of the Mendel Gottesman Library of Yeshiva University; the two of them create knowledge for a living, and spent much time with me in finding, discussing, and explaining sources.

I am quite certain that there will be errors in this book, due to the breadth that I have undertaken, moving from studies in comparative Semitic languages to anthropology, Greek and Kantian philosophy, biblical exegesis, and theology. If you, the reader, are willing to shine additional light on anything contained in the book, I would be most grateful.

Thank you also to everyone who got the inside joke that when I decided to establish a publishing house I would call it "Kodesh" Press. The name was a constant reminder to me that while I am extremely privileged to work with many talented and erudite authors, I also had an additional purpose, which was to complete my own study project.

Thank you most especially to my beloved wife, Caroline. Your support and encouragement have allowed me to finally complete a project that has been ten years in the making. Every day married to you is a pleasure, adventure, and privilege, and I am overjoyed to be going through life with you.

Alec Goldstein
New York, NY
November 2018

Introduction

Yet there remains with us the feeling that all poetry and all intellectual life were once the handmaids of the holy, and have passed through the temple.

— Jacob Burckhardt[1]

To my knowledge, the Jewish idea of holiness has not yet received a proper study. Such a study is daunting, since the word appears in multiple contexts, including narrative, jurisprudence, theology, and poetry. Although authors of all religions have addressed the notion of holiness, no work traces its meanings from pre-biblical times until today. This work follows the meanings of the Hebrew root *ḳ-d-sh*, "holy," using biblical passages, extra-biblical texts, as well as rabbinic literature, to modern times.

One of the most challenging tasks is to tease out the numerous sources about holiness that are familiar to most readers, such as Rashi's comment that *ḳedoshim tihyu*, "you shall be holy" (Lev. 19:2) means *hevu perushim*, "be separate"; or the concept from Nahmanides that holiness means one should not be a *naval bi-reshut ha-Torah*, a "glutton who

1. Burckhardt 1943: 148.

persists within the confines of Torah law"; Isaiah's trisagion "holy, holy, holy" (Isa. 6:3), the talmudic dictum *ḳaddesh atzmekha be-muttar lakh*, "sanctify yourself [even] in what is permitted you"; Rudolf Otto's *mysterium tremendum*; Rabbi Joseph B. Soloveitchik's *ein ḳedushah beli hakhanah*, "there is no holiness without preparation"[2]; and Warren Zev Harvey's exposition that holiness is a command to *imitatio dei*. To determine the relationship of these sources may demand the reader to reassess familiar sources, while never suspending the ability to reason critically.

Traditional Sources

This study will analyze how the root *ḳ-d-sh* is used in traditional sources: the Tanakh (Hebrew Bible), the Talmud, and the Medieval commentaries. These sources represent the backbone, tradition, and grandeur of Jewish thought. However, there are few systematic analyses of holiness among medieval Jewish authorities (Nahmanides being the notable exception), which means that much of the medieval material must be pieced together from their various writings.

Rudolf Otto

Besides the traditional Jewish sources, there are several works worthy of summary before proceeding. The most famous work on holiness is probably *The Idea of the Holy* by Rudolf Otto. Otto's greatest contribution to the theological lexicon is the word "numinous." He writes, "*Omen* has given us 'ominous,'

---

2. Perhaps based on Nahmanides, "man's [reward in] life for the observance of the commandments is in accordance with his preparation for them" (on Lev. 18:4).

and there is no reason why from *numen* we should not similarly form a word 'numinous'" (1958: 7). The Latin word *nūmen* means "divine will, divinity," from which derives the English cognate, "numen," meaning, "Deity, divinity, divine or presiding power or spirit" (*Oxford English Dictionary*). Otto, however, was not the first author to use an adjectival form of "numen," and the *Oxford English Dictionary* traces the first use of "numinous" to 1647.

One of the problems with Otto's thesis is that by his own admission, numinous "cannot be strictly defined" (p. 7). In other words, despite his best efforts, the word "numinous" is only of limited usefulness to understanding holiness as an overall concept.

Mircea Eliade

Another work that addresses holiness is Mircea Eliade's *The Sacred and the Profane*. Where Otto approached holiness from a phenomenological perspective, Eliade's focus was anthropological. He writes, "Otto undertook to analyze the modalities of *the religious experience*" (1959: 8, emphasis original). Eliade responded with an anthropological excursus which describes how early religions related to the holy. Where Otto sought to analyze, within a limited scope, the religious experience in nineteenth-century Protestant Germany and some eastern creeds, Eliade was more concerned with primeval religious behavior.

Eliade forms a neologism of his own, "hierophany," a portmanteau from the Greek, whose meaning is "to reveal the sacred," which he defines as "the *act of manifestation* of the sacred" (p. 11). Eliade explains:

It is impossible to overemphasize the paradox represented by every hierophany, even the most elementary. By manifesting the sacred, any object becomes *something else*, yet it continues to remain *itself*, for it continues to participate in its surrounding cosmic milieu. A *sacred* stone remains a *stone*; apparently (or, more precisely, from the profane point of view), nothing distinguishes it from all other stones. But for those to who a stone reveals itself as sacred, its immediate reality is transmuted into a supernatural reality. In other words, for those who have a religious experience all nature is capable of revealing itself as cosmic sacrality. The cosmos in its entirety can become a hierophany (p. 12, emphasis original).

"Hierophany" is the existence of something in two realms: the physical existence in the mundane realm, and the metaphysical existence where an object is devoted to some sacred purpose.[3]

The twentieth-century theologian Paul Tillich writes, very similarly, that any object in existence can manifest the holy "if we consider them not objects of a cognitive approach but elements of an encounter, namely, an encounter with the holy." Tillich does not use the word "theophany," but spends several pages developing the theme that anything at all can be an interaction with holiness (1955: 24). This concern with

---

3. The original French edition, *Le sacré et le profane*, appeared in 1957, which was translated in 1959. In 1966, the word *hierophany* was used by Thomas Pynchon in *The Crying of Lot 49*, "Some immediacy was there again, some promise of hierophany..." (Pynchon 1966: 20).

the manifestation of holiness appears to be Tillich's ultimate concern with the order of the universe, what he calls "ontology."

Eliade also focuses on how holiness is relevant today. Primitive man once possessed certain thoughts and feelings, and performed special actions, relating to holy objects. Today, according to Eliade, even the most committed atheists who seek to expunge religion from all aspects of life cannot overcome their own innate religious nature. Weddings, births, and funerals—once surrounded by religious ritual—remain ceremonial and emotionally evocative. This emotional response to these "successive initiations" shows how even ancient notions of holiness remain present, though sometimes buried, in modern society.

Jacob Milgrom

Jacob Milgrom's *chef d'oeuvre* is a three-volume commentary on Leviticus (1991-1999), and he also wrote a commentary on the book of Numbers (1990), as well as numerous scholarly articles. Milgrom received his rabbinic ordination from the Jewish Theological Seminary and some of of Milgrom's conclusions are highly problematic from an Orthodox Jewish perspective. However, other comments of his are remarkably insightful, so Milgrom is a tremendous resource that must be utilized cautiously.

Milgrom's writing breathes life back into Leviticus, a book that many readers today find antiquated. However, the importance of Leviticus to understanding holiness cannot be overstated, since that book contains the root *k-d-sh* more than any other biblical book, so I have relied heavily on Milgrom while eschewing the parts that are inconsistent with traditional Jewish belief.

Mary Douglas

Mary Douglas has produced another influential anthropological work, *Purity and Danger*. Two of her insights are worth noting here. First, she frequently writes that there is no such thing as dirt. Each society creates its own definition of cleanness and uncleanness. (A recurring theme will be that *purity* is a prerequisite for *holiness*.) Each definition of cleanness and uncleanness—of dirt—is societal, and each society defines "dirt" as what is anomalous from the norm. However, Milgrom quotes from Anna Meigs that this theory must be somewhat limited, since while "many phenomena are out of place only a few are pollutants" (Milgrom 1991: 721).

Second, according to Douglas, laws of purity and holiness (she seldom distinguishes between the two) often relate to what traverses the orifices of the body, either entering or exiting. Holiness often has restrictions and boundaries—a liminality—about it.[4] Being holy, even in Judaism, is often about what traverses the mouth and the genitalia, the two most lustful orifices of the human form. For example, Maimonides, in his *Sefer Ḳedushah*, "Book of [the laws of] Holiness," compiles the laws of forbidden sexual relations and prohibited foods.

Although Douglas has some useful insights, she has also been rightly and harshly criticized. Milgrom writes, "her biblical comments, especially in her early writings, are replete with errors," and further she "cites a host of wrong or

---

4. Gorman quotes many authorities that use words such as "liminal" and "marginal," especially as rites of passage (1990: 53).

nonexistent verses" (1991: 721). Milgrom presents a litany of factual errors (not errors in interpretation), which forces the serious reader to question Douglas' reliability in scholarly circles. In fact, Douglas herself admits that she wrote *Purity and Danger* without having read the book of Numbers (2002: xv), which deals with such central topics as the sacred status of the Nazirite as well as the purification of the Levites.

In fact, the title of her work already betrays her ignorance: *Purity and Danger*. "Purity" and "danger" are not antithetical notions. Holy objects and places are sometimes dangerous to someone who is not properly sanctified, but that risk concerns holiness, not purity. Her failure to distinguish between purity and holiness is a major oversight of her work, especially since the difference between them is so fundamental to understanding Semitic religions.

John Gammie

John G. Gammie has produced a short but insightful work, *Holiness in Israel*, on the Hebrew Bible and the Apocrypha. He has divided holiness among the priestly, prophetic, and sapiental passages in the Bible (1989: 1-2). These categories are useful, as even the most casual reader will notice that Leviticus and Isaiah use the word "holy" in wildly different ways. And, surprisingly, in wisdom literature like Job and Proverbs, the root *k-d-sh* seldom appears.[5] Nonetheless, Gammie observes "a unity with a diversity," reminding the reader that if we accept the Bible as true—and ultimately, therefore, cohesive—

---

5. Thrice in Proverbs (9:10, 20:25, and 30:3), and five times in Job (1:5, 5:1, 6:10, 15:15, 26:14). Similarly, holiness is conspicuously absent from *Avot*.

we cannot view each category's definition as exhaustive or mutually exclusive. At some point, the priestly, prophetic, and sapiential relationships must unite in order to achieve an integrated understanding of biblical holiness.

Other Materials

Needless to say, there are many other books, commentaries, articles, and excerpts—some very broad and some very narrow in scope—on which I have drawn. Those materials will be presented over the duration of the work.

Now let us begin.

Chapter 1

Proposed Etymologies of *Ḳ-D-SH*

… there is no surer or more illuminating way of reading a man's character, and perhaps a little of his past history, than by observing the contexts in which he prefers to use certain words.

— Owen Barfield[6]

The root *ḳ-d-sh* is a popular Semitic root that appears in numerous languages, including Akkadian, Aramaic, Ge'ez, Hebrew, Phoenician/Punic, and Ugaritic.[7] Yet although *ḳ-d-sh* is attested

---

6. Barfield 1967: 163.

7. For Northwest Semitic generally, see *Dictionary of North-West Semitic Inscriptions* 993-997. For Akkadian: *CAD* Q 46-47. For Aramaic: *ḳ-d-sh* is attested in Biblical Aramaic (*HALOT* 1968; *BDB* 111), in Rabbinic Aramaic (Jastrow 1319-1321; Sokoloff [Bab.] 987-988; Sokoloff [Pal.] 476-477), in the Dead Sea Scrolls (Vogt 2008: 286) and in external sources (Cook 1974: 103). For Ge'ez, see Leslau 422-423. For Hebrew: *ḳ-d-sh* is attested in Biblical Hebrew (*HALOT* 1072-1078; *BDB* 871-874), Ben Sira (e.g., Beentjes 1997: 31), Qumran Hebrew (e.g., *DCH* 7:190-204), Rabbinic Hebrew (Jastrow 1319-1321), and Modern Hebrew (Alcalay 2239-2242). For Phoenician/Punic, see Krahmalkov 2000: 425-426. For Ugaritic, see Del Olmo Lete 2003: 695-697.

in all Semitic languages, its etymology has remained a mystery. We will examine several proposed meanings of the root.

K̦-D-SH & Separation

Many rabbinic authorities explain that *k̦-d-sh* originally meant "separated."[8] There is biblical evidence for this position, when *k̦-d-sh* is used with other, broader, words for "separated." One example is the verse, "And you shall be holy [*k̦-d-sh*] to Me; for I the Lord am holy, and I have set you apart [*b-d-l*] from the nations to be Mine" (Lev. 20:26). There are also rabbinic statements that seem to equate the root *k̦-d-sh* with other roots for separation:

> Rabbi Judah b. Pazzi said: Why did Scripture juxtapose the passage of forbidden sexual acts (Leviticus 18) with the passage of holiness (Leviticus 19)? To teach you that whoever separates [*p-r-sh*] from forbidden relations is called "holy" (JT *Yevamot* 12a [2:4]; cf. *Leviticus Rabbah* 24:6).

> It is written here, "And I shall be sanctified [*k̦-d-sh*] among the children of Israel" (Lev. 22:32) and it is written there, "Separate [*b-d-l*] yourselves from among this congregation" (*Berakhot* 21b, *Sanhedrin* 74a; quoting Num. 16:21).

> The Holy One, Blessed be He, said to Moses: Go say unto My children Israel, "Just as I am separated [*p-r-sh*],

---

8. As this development unfolds, it may become clear that "separation" *from what* differs among the sources.

so you shall be separated [*p-r-sh*]. Just as I am holy [*k-d-sh*], so you shall be holy [*k-d-sh*]." This is what is written, "You shall be holy [*k-d-sh*]" (*Leviticus Rabbah* 23:4; also Rashi on Lev. 19:2 and Nahmanides on 21:6).

Three medieval Hebrew dictionaries have also codified that *k-d-sh* means "separated." The tenth-century lexicographer Menahem ben Saruk says the root *k-d-sh* is "divided into three meanings," representing favorable separation, neutral separation, and unfavorable separation. Jonah ibn Janah (d. 1050) seems to take a similar approach, although he does not explicitly identify three distinct meanings. R. David Kimhi (1160-1235), in his *Sefer ha-Shorashim*, seems to identify the same three meanings that Menahem invoked, although without composing a formal list. In the nineteenth century, Dr. Alexander Kohut, in his *Aruch Completum*, defined *k-d-sh* as *perishah ve-hevdel*, "separateness and distinctiveness."

The two modern authoritative dictionaries of Biblical Hebrew are far less certain about this meaning than their medieval counterparts; yet both do identify an original meaning of separation. First, *The Brown-Driver-Briggs Hebrew and English Lexicon* (*BDB*) writes, "poss. orig. of *separation, withdrawal*" (p. 871). *BDB* offers no theories about the etymology, but quotes several earlier authorities who define *k-d-sh* as "separation." Koehler-Baumgartner's *The Hebrew & Aramaic Lexicon of the Old Testament* (*HALOT*) defines *k-d-sh* as "an original verb, which can only with difficulty be traced back to a root קד 'to cut'; if this is the case the basic meaning of קדשׁ would be 'to set apart'...."

Ḳ-D-SH & Purity

Keil & Delitzsch believe *ḳ-d-sh* is related to *ḥ-d-sh*, which they define as "splendid, pure," in which case the root *ḳ-d-sh* is related to the idea of purity. In Akkadian, a language that flourished in the ancient Near East for approximately the last three millennia before the Common Era, the verb *quddušu* means "to clean" or "to make ritually clean."[9] *BDB* quotes Meissner's opinion that *ḳ-d-sh* means "cleanse." There is even one place in the Bible where the Hebrew root *ḳ-d-sh* almost certainly means "purify": "And David sent messengers and took her, and she came to him, and he lay with her, and she was purifying herself [*mitḳaddeshet*] from her uncleanness…" (2 Sam. 11:4).

There are other verses where different commentators see *ḳ-d-sh* as purity, e.g., Nahmanides on Exod. 19:10 (also Sarna 1986:131), Rashi on 2 Chron. 29:17. There is also a Ugaritic text *b'l qdšm b nhr*, which is translated ambiguously as "Baal sanctified [purified?] them in the river."

Ḳ-D-SH & Newness

A Standard Bible Dictionary, edited by Melancthon W. Jacobus, Jr., writes that "*qōdhesh*, is derived from a root kindred to that which means 'newness' (*ḥādhash*…)." According to this, *ḳ-d-sh* comes from *ḥ-d-sh*, which this source defines as "new, renewed" (as opposed to Kiel & Delitzch's understanding of *ḥ-d-sh* as "splendid, pure"). Conceptually, something may

---

9. *CAD* Q, defs. 2-3. Van der Toorn also writes, "The principal connotation of *qadāšu* is 'purity,' though in the restricted sense of ritual purity" (1985: 28).

be considered holy if the object is renewed, proverbially or physically, to a deity.[10] The gap between "pure" and "renewed" may not be terribly large, since something new or renewed is often considered pure and unmolested.

There is some rationale to identify *k-d-sh* with *h-d-sh*, since they share the two final root letters. Keil & Delitzsch said it might even be related to the Sanskrit *dhûsch*, meaning "splendid, beautiful." There is also a famous line from Rabbi Abraham Isaac Kook: *ha-yashan yithaddash ve-ha-hadash yitkaddash*, "the old shall be renewed and the new shall be sanctified." Nonetheless, the identification of *k-d-sh* with *h-d-sh* is tenuous since these words tend to have limited interaction in texts, and seem to belong to different fields. Also, there is serious scholarly debate whether the *kof* (ק) and *het* (ח) are prone to interchange.[11]

K-D-Sh & Fire

There is a rabbinic etymology that *k-d-sh* means "surrendered to fire," based on the verse, "You shall not sow your vineyard with two kinds of seed; *pen tikdash* the entirety of what you have planted" (Deut. 22:9). One rabbinic dictum reinterprets the consonantal form *pen tikdash* as *pen tukad esh*, "lest it [become liable to] be burnt in a fire" (*Kiddushin* 56b, *Hullin* 115a).

---

10. There is also an inscription which reads *hydš w'yqdš*, "he has renewed and consecrated" (*DNWSI* 993, quoting *KAI* 138:6).

11. Ringgren writes, "the shift *q/h* has not been demonstrated" (*TDOT* 523), but Muillenburg sees a connection between *kof* and *het*, e.g., *k-tz-b/h-tz-b*, *k-tz-p/h-tz-p*, and *k-tz-r/h-tz-r* (1962: 617).

Although this interpretation is generally not accepted, Samuel David Luzzatto (Shadal) believed it was the true origin of the word, and wrote "that the term originally applied to sacrifices that were burned in order to honor God. Later the term was transferred to anything that was set aside for God's honor and removed from profane use, even if no burning was involved" (on Exod. 15:11).

Several texts from Gudea, King of Lagash (reigned c. 2144-2124 B.C.E.), also discuss consecration by fire: "Its foundation he made holy, with fire he laid" (Wilson 1994: 35). According to this Sumerian rite, fire was kindled to signal the city's sanctity; Shadal suggested that it referred to things that were completely consumed in honor to God. It is possible that the Sumerian rite is a religious synecdoche, where kindling a fire within the city symbolizes a full immolation to the gods. Holiness is also mentioned alongside fire elsewhere in Tanakh, but these contexts seem unrelated (Isa. 10:17, Ezek. 28:14).

Ḳ-D-SH as an Original Root

Propp seems to believe ḳ-d-sh is an original three-letter root, meaning "to be numinous, imbued with a divine quality" (1999: 200). Clines also writes that ḳ-d-sh "is a term for the deity's status or quality (i.e. God is holy), and what belongs to or is in the realm of the deity" (n.d., 14-15). After all, the idea of holiness is—according to many authorities—a concept *sui generis* and irreducible to any other, so we should not assume we can trace its etymology to another concept. Alternatively, holiness might be a placeholder term for "godlike" or "related to a deity," which would again be a term very different from the proposed etymologies above. I find it much more likely that *ḳ-d-sh* is a bona fide three-letter root rather than trying to trace it to alternative words.[12]

---

12. Several attestations of the root *ḳ-d-sh* are used to refute the theory that this root carries primarily a sacral meaning. First, "You shall not sow your vineyard with two kinds of seed; lest the entirety of what you have planted be *ḳ-d-sh* together with whatever else comes from [that] vineyard" (Deut. 22:9). Onkelos and Rashi understand this use of *ḳ-d-sh* as separation by degradation/demotion. However, the Dead Sea Scrolls (4Q MMT B 77-79), Septuagint, and probably Josephus (*Antiquities* 4:208) understand the verse as referring to holiness. Milgrom also writes, "it will belong not to you, but to the sanctuary" (2000: 1663). There is at least a *prima facie* argument that *pen tiḳdash* is used combatively against a heathen practice, which would have consisted of growing wheat and wine together.

Second, the phrase "*ḳ-d-sh* war" is usually translated "prepare war" (Jer. 6:4, 51:27-28, Joel 4:9, Mic. 3:5). However, war has a sacral component, since its preparations consisted of "holy vessels and trumpets" (Num. 31:7), consultation with the Urim and Thummim (1 Sam. 28:6), and abstention from unsanctified food (1 Sam. 21:4-7). The "holiness" could also be a reference to sexual restraint (Deut. 23:15, on which Nahmanides adds, "the entire camp is like the Sanctuary of God"), or an eschatological holy war. The end of battle was also marked by *ḥērem* (Joshua 7).

Additional difficult examples: the word *kedeishah* is often translated "prostitute," but might have originally referred to a cultic functionary; the fasting and assembling mentioned in Joel (1:14, 2:15-16) can have an obvious sacral component; and Jeremiah is called "sanctified" by God for his sacred mission of rebuking the nation (Jer. 1:5). Nahmanides understands many of these difficult attestations in terms of a meaning of "holiness" (see on Deut. 23:18).

Chapter 2

Lexical Analysis I: Types of Separation

One feels that in theologians' hands they are only a set of
titles obtained by a mechanical manipulation of synonyms.

— William James

It is true that *part* of the meaning of *ḳ-d-sh* is "separated"
or something similar, but that is not the whole meaning. In
linguistics, this is called componential analysis, which is an
assessment of "the total meaning of a word being seen in terms
of a number of distinct elements or components of meaning"
(Palmer 1976: 108). For example, "man" can be defined
as "human + adult + male," "woman" as "human + adult +
female," and "child" as "human + young." It is my theory
that in general the root *ḳ-d-sh*, "holy," has two *components*:
"separated" and "elevated."

Even authorities who supply the component "separated"
do not accept that as the fullness of the word. As quoted
above, Menahem ben Saruk believes *ḳ-d-sh* is "divided into
three groups." In the first category, "elevation," he quotes,
"There is none holy [*ḳ-d-sh*] as the Lord" (1 Sam. 2:2). In the

second category, he quotes, "declare [k-d-sh] a fast and call for war" (Joel 1:14), and other examples of what he believes are examples of what might be called "horizontal separation." In the third category, which could be called "separation by demotion," he quotes, "There shall be no prostitute [k-d-sh] among the daughters of Israel" (Deut. 23:17). In this, Menahem is the most articulate advocate that k-d-sh has this three-part meaning, and his formulation is quoted nearly verbatim by Rashi (on Deut. 22:9).

Yet Menahem is not the first authority to claim k-d-sh has a tripartite meaning. Onkelos, the official Aramaic translation of the Pentateuch dating from the first century, also includes all three meanings—i.e., separation by elevation, horizontal separation, and separation by demotion. As an example of horizontal separation, Onkelos translates ve-kiddashtam (Exod. 19:10) as u-tezammeninnun, from the root z-m-n, which means "and you shall prepare." As an example of separation by degradation, he translates pen tikdash (Deut. 22:9) as dilma tista'ev, which means "lest it become defiled," from the root s-'-b (סאב).

This section will show how the root k-d-sh has been associated with other Hebrew roots for "separation" or similar concepts. Some Hebrew words commonly associated with k-d-sh are:

- Hebrew b-d-l, "separate,"
- Hebrew p-r-sh, "separate, distinguish,"
- Hebrew n-t-n, "give, give over,"
- Hebrew h-n-k, "inaugurate,"

- Hebrew *k-v-n*, "ready, get ready,"
- Hebrew *z-m-n*, "prepare,"
- Hebrew *t-h-r*, "purify."

Ḳ-D-SH and Separation (*B-D-L* and *P-R-SH*)

Holiness is often compared to the idea of separation in its simplest form; in Hebrew, this is represented by the roots *b-d-l* and *p-r-sh*. For example, "And you shall be holy [*k-d-sh*] unto Me; for I the Lord am holy, and I have set you apart [*b-d-l*] from the nations to be Mine" (Lev. 20:26; see *Berakhot* 21b and *Sanhedrin* 74a). Additionally, Maimonides writes that through the dietary and sexual laws, "the Omnipresent has sanctified us [*k-d-sh*] and separated us [*b-d-l*] from the nations" (*Mishneh Torah*, "Peratei ha-Sefarim").

The concept of separation is also represented by the Hebrew root *p-r-sh*, "make distinct, declare." The Hebrew root *p-r-sh* probably represents a more specific type of separation than *b-d-l*. Cognate with Akkadian *parāšu*, Hebrew *p-r-sh* probably means separating or cutting after measurement and consideration. On the verse *ḳedoshim tihyu*, "you shall be holy" (Lev. 19:2), sources comment that the meaning is *perishah* (JT *Yevamot* 12a, *Leviticus Rabbah* 23:4, Rashi). Nahmanides also says that *ḳedushah* is represented by *perishut* (see Lev. 21:6).[13]

Other sources take issue with this understanding, and say that distinction (*perishah*) is a necessary precondition for

13. Full citation: "Holiness signifies separateness, as I have explained in the section above [on Lev. 19:2]. Scripture is thus stating that even in those things which are permissible to Israelites, the priests should exercise self-control, avoiding the impurity of the dead, and marrying of women who are unfit for them in purity and cleanness."

holiness (*kedushah*), but it is not the fullness of the concept. Rabbi S.R. Hirsch writes, "separation [*p-r-sh*] is not yet holiness [*k-d-sh*], but it is a preliminary stage towards it" (on Lev. 19:2). Similarly, Warren Zev Harvey writes, "*kadosh* is partially synonymous with *parush* ('separated') and *nivdal* ('distinct')" (1977: 9) and further asserts, "although *kedushah* seems necessarily to involve separation, separation does not necessarily involve *kedushah*" (12). Rabbi Hirsch's use of "preliminary stage" and Harvey's "partially synonymous" correspond with the componential analysis conducted above. The root *k-d-sh* has the semantic component of *b-d-l* or *p-r-sh*, but *k-d-sh* is a more developed specific type of separation.

K-D-SH and Transferring (*N-T-N*)

In at least four cases the root *k-d-sh* is used in relation to the verb *n-t-n* ("give, give over"):

- In regards to Jermiah's designation as a prophet, the verbs *k-d-sh* and *n-t-n* are used consecutively: "Before I formed you in the belly I knew you, and before you came forth out of the womb I sanctified [*k-d-sh*] you; I have given [*n-t-n*] you as a prophet to the nations" (Jer. 1:5).
- The Israelites are commanded to set aside the firstborn to God. The Torah usually uses the verb *k-d-sh* (Exod. 13:2, Num. 3:12-13, Deut. 15:19), yet in one verse uses the verb *n-t-n*, "give" (Exod. 22:28).
- Regarding the cities of refuge, the verb *n-t-n* is used at Josh. 20:2, but regarding the specific city of refuge named Kadesh, the verb *k-d-sh* is used (Josh. 20:7). The latter verse is used

as evidence that *ḳ-d-sh* has a primary non-sacral meaning. However, S.D. Luzzatto writes, "... it is true that it would have been proper to use the verb *va-yavdilu*... but it seems that out of a preference for plays on words, it was written *va-yakdishu et Kedesh*. In any case, the term *kedushah* is well employed with respect to cities of refuge, for the refuge given to manslayers was originally a distinction unique to sanctuaries and altars" (on Exod. 15:11).

- The most striking example is that the biblical priests are sanctified using the verb *ḳ-d-sh* (e.g., *ve-ḳiddashta otam*, "and you shall sanctify them" — Exod. 28:41), while the Levites are appointed with the phrase *ve-natattah et ha-Levi'im*, "and you shall give over [*n-t-n*] the Levites" (Num. 3:9). It is a subtle but powerful argument that this variation is intentional. Jacob Milgrom writes, "This distinction is consistently maintained... thereby emphasizing that only the priests—but never the Levites—are authorized to have access to the most sacred sancta" (1990:17). Both *n-t-n* and *ḳ-d-sh* suggest a change in ownership, but *n-t-n* is a broader term.

Ḳ-D-SH and Initiation (*Ḥ-N-Ḳ*)

The root *ḳ-d-sh* is sometimes used with the root *ḥ-n-k*, as in the verse, "so the king and all the children of Israel *ḥ-n-k*-ed the house of the Lord. On the same day, the king sanctified [*ḳ-d-sh*] the middle of the court that was before the house of the Lord" (1 Kings 8:63-64; cf. 2 Chron. 7:4-8). To this extent, Baruch Levine notes that "*kiddesh*, 'to consecrate' often figures in the initial dedication of sacred places and persons" (1989: 106).

There is considerable debate about the meaning of the root
ḥ-n-k. A few theories include:

- Rashi understands it as *hathallah*, "beginning, initiation"
  (on Gen. 14:14 and Deut. 20:5). Rashi's opinion is based
  on the fact that *ḥ-n-k* is used in reference to private houses
  (Deut. 20:5) and children (Prov. 22:6), where no obvious
  sacral component exists. Rashi's opinion is also favored by
  Jacob Milgrom (1991: 592-595).[14]

- Maimonides believes *inyan ha-ḥinnukh ha-hergel*, "the
  meaning of *ḥ-n-k* is habit [or regularity, constancy]." He
  continues, *ve-hush'alah millat 'ḥinnukh' bi-devarim eilah
  le-hathallat ha-asiyah*, explaining *ḥ-n-k* means "initiation"
  only as an extended, secondary meaning (see *PhM Menaḥot*
  4:4).

- Menachem Zvi Kaddari defines *ḥ-n-k* as *hakdashat
  binyan o mivne' le-tafkido*, "sanctification of a building or
  structure for its purpose." *BDB* gives a secondary meaning
  of "dedicate, consecrate." Furthermore, the English word
  "dedicate" is fundamentally a synonym of "consecrate,"[15]
  so translating *ḥ-n-k* as "dedicate" (as KJV and NRSV do) is
  to posit a sacred meaning to the Hebrew.

---

14. This is also probably the opinion of Even-Shoshan in his
Concordance, despite his use of the root *k-d-sh* in some of his
explanations.

15. The English word "dedicate" has historically been a synonym
of "consecrate," i.e., it has a fundamentally sacred meaning. The
sacred component of "dedicate" is identified by Samuel Johnson
(eighteenth century), the *OED* (nineteenth century), and *American
Heritage 5* (twentieth century).

The use of *ḥ-n-k* for religious sites like temples, altars, and city walls emphasizes the newness of the place, not its sanctity; the sanctity is from the use of *ḳ-d-sh*. Reif noted, "Such initiations would naturally represent ideal opportunities for celebrations and festivities but they are not to be confused with dedication or consecration ceremonies" (1972:497). But initiation and dedication are two different ideas, represented by two different Hebrew words. Initiation is *ḥ-n-k*; dedication (i.e., consecration) is *ḳ-d-sh*.

Ḳ-D-SH and Preparation (*K-V-N* and *Z-M-N*)

Many sources relate holiness to the concept of preparation, which is represented in Hebrew by *k-v-n* (as in *le-hakhin, hakhanah*), "establish, set up, be ready," and *z-m-n*, "prepare."[16] The ideas of preparation and holiness are clear in the verses, "Go to the people and sanctify [*ḳ-d-sh*] them today and tomorrow, and let them wash their garments. And they shall be ready [*k-v-n*]..." (Exod. 19:10-11). Other texts that compare the idea of holiness and preparation include:

- "the Lord has prepared [*hekhin*] a sacrifice, He has *hiḳdish* His guests" (Zeph. 1:7),
- "And the vessels... we have prepared [*hekhannu*] and sanctified [*ve-hiḳdashnu*]" (2 Chron. 29:19).

---

16. The Semitic root *z-m-n* is an Aramaism, appearing in Biblical Hebrew both late and seldom, and there are no biblical verses where *ḳ-d-sh* and *z-m-n* are used seriatim. Nonetheless, there are numerous diachronic sources that interpret *ḳ-d-sh* as *z-m-n*.

The relationship between holiness and preparation is further developed by the root *z-m-n*. For example, Onkelos translates the Hebrew words *k-d-sh* and *k-v-n* with the Aramaic root *z-m-n*, "Go to the people and sanctify [*k-d-sh*; Onkelos, *z-m-n*] them.... And they shall be ready [*nekhonim*, from *k-v-n*; Onkelos *z-m-n*]..." (Exod. 19:10-11). Rashi follows Onkelos, writing Moses "shall prepare [*z-m-n*] them, that they shall be ready [*k-v-n*]."[17]

As quoted by Rabbi Herschel Schachter, Rabbi Joseph B. Soloveitchik solidifies this thematic connection: "'And sanctify them today and tomorrow' (Exod. 19:10). Onkelos translates this, 'prepare them,' since there is no holiness without preparation" (2010: 274). Apparently the saying, "There is no holiness without preparation" was a popular slogan at Yeshiva University when Rabbi Soloveitchik taught there. Signs bearing this phrase in Hebrew (*ein kedushah beli hakhanah*) were hung over many study halls and classrooms throughout the university. These banners inculcated the students with a sense of diligence and preparation to properly understand the Torah and its teachings.[18]

One philosophical difference between separation (*b-d-l* and *p-r-sh*) and preparation (*k-v-n* and *z-m-n*) is timing. To compare the relationship of separation vis-à-vis preparation is important; if the stress is on the separation, then the sanctification occurs coincident with the separation. If the stress is laid on the preparation, then the sanctification process begins at an earlier stage.

---

17. Tosafot also understands *mekuddeshet* in the context of betrothal as *mezummenet* (*Kiddushin* 2a, s.v. *de-asar*).

18. While I have heard about these banners from several sources, I have not been able to locate a photograph.

Ḳ-D-SH and Purity (*T-H-R*)

A seventh root associated with *ḳ-d-sh* is *t-h-r*, "pure." Anthropologically, one must distinguish between the concepts "purity" and "holiness." To this end, W. Robertson Smith, the founder of modern comparative religion, writes: "Primarily, purification means the application to the person of some medium which removes a taboo, and enables the person purified to mingle freely in the ordinary life of his fellows. It is not therefore identical with consecration, for the latter often brings special taboos with it" (1889: 425).[19] Milgrom updates the terminology, and instead of calling the defilements "taboo," refers to them as "pollutants" (e.g., 1991: 721). The state of impurity brings corresponding restriction; for example, people who are impure may not partake of holy offerings or tread in holy places. Removal of this impurity—what we would call "purification," or the act of making pure—permits one to interact with society as before, and without restriction. The act of *sanctification* is a subsequent process that, in the ancient Near East as well as in the Bible, cannot be achieved until after purification.

The most common Hebrew word for "pure" is *t-h-r*, which in Ugaritic, a language spoken in biblical times in what is now Syria, is a secular root meaning "shining, [physically] pure."[20]

---

19. In Josephine Tey's *The Daughter of Time*, a bed-ridden hospital patient requests that his bed be moved from its present location, yet his request is denied, because "in hospitals symmetry ranked just a short head behind cleanliness and a whole length in front of Godliness" (11).

20. The dictionaries debate this point. Murtonen defines Ugaritic *t-h-r* as "to be pure, (ritually) clean" (*Hebrew in its West Semitic Setting*), which posits a religious meaning. However, *Dictionary of*

Nahmanides writes, "the meaning of 'purity [*taharah*]' is 'cleanness' [*nikkayon*; root: *n-k-y*]' as in 'pure gold' (Exod. 25:39), smelted and refined [*tzaruf u-mezukkak*] as in 'And he shall sit as a refiner and purifier [*metzaref u-metaher*] of silver and he shall purify [*ve-tihar*] the sons of Levi and purge [*ve-zikkak*] them as gold and silver' (Mal. 3:3)" (on Lev. 12:4). Chavel adds that Nahmanides understood *taharah* to mean cleanness "in a physical sense."

In Biblical Hebrew, *t-h-r* possesses an additional, religious meaning, referring to ritual purity. Some other Semitic words for purity may have experienced a similar development.[21] The

the Ugaritic Language defines it as a secular root, "sparkling, pure," which seems to be the favored definition. Similarly, Levine writes "the root *t-h-r* has as its primary connotation, a physical purity" (Levine 1989: 106). Jastrow also sees that *t-h-r* was originally a secular root, "to be bright, to glitter," but biblically also means, "to be clean, pure, esp. to be levitically clean" (Jastrow 1903: 520). It is likely that the secular meaning is original because, as Mitchell First observes, "Words normally have concrete meanings before they develop abstract meanings" (2015: 40 n. 41). It seems that the common Ugaritic words for ritual purity are *r-h-tz* and *b-r-r*, most notably when the king begins his temple duties, it is said *ytrhs mlk brr*, "the king shall wash himself clean."

21. Some additional Semitic words for purity are:

(1) *z-k*, which may have originally meant "innocent" from wrongdoing (see Job 33:9). This is the second most common word for "purity," from Akkadian *zakû*. I have seen no evidence that the word ז"ך (transliterated *z-k*) is related to זק"ק (transliterated *z-k-k*).

(2) *r-h-tz*, "wash, bathe," and is used metaphorically once (Ps. 60:10).

(3) *k-b-s*, which usually means "wash, launder clothes," especially in anticipation of an act of *t-h-r* (e.g., Lev. 14:80, which prompts the *Mekhilta* to write "there is no laundering

idea of religious purity likely has its origins as an outgrowth of physical cleanness. In a ritual sense, acts of purification describe the removal of something that is religiously or ritually undesirable, something that must be removed because it serves as a legal or spiritual impediment.

However, by modern standards, the words for "purity" and "holiness" were not preserved as rigorously as one might wish. For example, occasionally both Akkadian and Arabic use the same root for both ideas, and the use of *k-d-sh* at 2 Sam. 11:4 is generally understood to mean "purify," not "sanctify."

[*k-b-s*] without ritual immersion"), yet *k-b-s* is also used metaphorically as a term of repentance (e.g., Jer. 4:14, Jer. 2:22, Ps. 51:4, 9).

(4) *h-t-'*, which means "purify" as a privative (the forms *hittē'* and *hatta't*), hence a *hatta't* should be translated as a "purgation offering" (Milgrom 1991: 232, quoting Saadiah). Also the Talmud explains that a woman who has just given birth brings a *hatta't*, though she committed no sin, because she is ritually impure: "the sacrifices she brings permits her to eat sacred food, and is not for the purpose of atonement" (*Kereitot* 26a; see however *Canticles Rabbah* 5:1, which claims a *hatta't* is brought for an actual sin).

(5) *k-p-r*, which as a *kal* means "wipe away" (e.g., the Shurpu ritual, where the sin is "wiped away" [tab. I, line 23], from Akkadian *kapāru*; see Geller 1980: 181-192). In the *pi'el*, it means "completely destroy" impurity (ritually, e.g., Lev. 4:26, and then metaphorically, e.g., Isa. 6:5-7). Rashi says it means *kinnuah*, and Malbim says it means *kissui*, "covering" (on Isa. 47:11). Rabbi Joseph B. Soloveitchik translates it as "acquittal" (Peli 1980: 57). (Rabbi Soloveitchik distinguishes between *kapparah*, "acquittal from sin or atonement," and *taharah*, "catharsis or purification." The Modern Hebrew word for "catharsis" is either *katarzis* or *hitaharut*.)

(6) *l-b-n*, which literally means "white," is also used to signify purity, especially in a poetic or metaphorical sense, as in, "I shall be whiter than snow" (Ps. 51:9).

Even in places that "purity" and "holiness" are not said to be the same concept, they are used in parallelism: "And he shall sprinkle of the blood on it with his finger seven times, and purify [*t-h-r*] it and sanctify [*k-d-sh*] it from the impurities of the children of Israel" (Lev. 16:19). Here, the priest sprinkles blood on the altar to achieve both purification (*t-h-r*) and sanctification (*k-d-sh*). Rashi quotes that *t-h-r* and *k-d-sh* have different meanings: "He shall purify it from [the sins] of the past, and he shall sanctify it [for use] in the future."[22] Purification removes prior impurities, and sanctification makes the altar suitable for future service. This reasoning is consistent with Smith's distinction between purity and holiness. Milgrom writes similarly, "Impurity and holiness must be kept apart at all costs.... Thus an object must first be emptied of its impurities before it may be sanctified. This necessitates two discrete processes: first decontamination and then consecration" (1991: 524).[23]

---

22. See also the *Yoma* 59a and Rashi, s.v. *ba-makom she-kiddesho*, which suggests that *t-h-r* and *k-d-sh* refer to two different actions. "Purification" and "sanctification" refer to two different rites which achieve two different spiritual goals.

23. Rabbi Hayyim Angel also points to a shift between *k-d-sh* and *t-h-r* in sanctifying the altars of Exod. 29:37 and Ezek. 43:26. He writes, "In the building of the *mishkan*, the term *kedushah* (holiness) is used, whereas Ezekiel employs the term *taharah* (purity).... To sanctify something is to elevate it from a neutral state to a positive state. *Taharah* is the opposite of *tumah* (impurity), a negative state. To purify something is to elevate it from a negative state and restore its original neutral state—essentially to make it regular *hullin* again" (Angel 2013: 67-68).

Interpretations of Exod. 19:10

A deeper look at Exod. 19:10 will show how different authorities integrate translation, exegesis, and theology around the root *ḳ-d-sh*. Exodus 19 discusses the preparation for the revelation at Sinai and the receiving of the Ten Commandments. The verse under current consideration is: "And the Lord said to Moses: Go to the people and *ḳ-d-sh* them today and tomorrow, and let them wash their garments" (Exod. 19:10).

Many commentaries understand *ḳ-d-sh* here as "prepare." For example, Onkelos and Rashi understand this usage as *z-m-n*. Similarly, Keil & Delitzsch also write, "God then commanded Moses to *prepare* the people for His appearing or speaking to them" (emphasis added).

A second way to understand *ḳ-d-sh* in this verse is "purify." This approach is taken by the Septuagint, "and *purify* them today and tomorrow, and let them wash their clothes" (NETS), which is likely what prompts Philo of Alexandria to say, "the soul of the man who is about to receive sacred laws should be thoroughly cleansed and purified from all stains" (*Decalogue* II.10). Rabbi David Kimhi also understands this as "purify" (on Ezek. 16:9).

Nahmanides also takes this approach, and he bases his argument on two factors. First, he quotes an ambiguous verse, "the priests had not *ḳ-d-sh*-ed themselves" (2 Chron. 30:2), where he says *ḳ-d-sh* means "purify." Nahmanides' second support for *ḳ-d-sh* meaning "purify" rather than "sanctify" is a statement from the *Mekhilta*: "there is no laundering of clothing without ritual immersion" (see also *Yevamot* 46b). Since Exod. 19:10 requires the Israelites to wash their clothes, they also needed to perform ritual immersion (*tevilah*, which is an act of purification). This is an argument *a fortiori*—if the clothing requires purification, then certainly the people themselves needed to be pure. Sarna provides a modern explanation, saying that the Israelites "had to maintain a state of purity, abstain from sexual relations, launder their clothes, and treat the mountain as strictly off-limits" (1986: 131).

A third interpretation is that *k-d-sh* in this verse literally means "sanctify." It is my opinion Maimonides took this interpretation, but this conclusion can only be determined by piecing together three passages. The first excerpt is, "There was immersion in the wilderness before giving the Torah, as it says, 'and *k-d-sh* them today and tomorrow, and let them wash their garments'" (*Issurei Bi'ah* 13:3). The second is, "Wherever it is said in the Torah 'washing flesh' or 'laundering garments' from impurities, this means immersion of the entire body in an immersion pool (*Mikva'ot* 1:2). The third, "God commanded [Moses] to sanctify the people for the receiving of the Law, and said, 'And *k-d-sh* them today and tomorrow' (Exod. 19:10), Moses [in obedience to this command] said to the people, 'Come not at your wives' (Exod. 19:15). Here it is clearly stated that sanctification consists in absence of sensuality (*Guide* 3:33).

Maimonides draws on the same *Mekhilta* that Nahmanides quoted, specifically that the Israelites needed to perform ritual immersion before receiving the Decalogue. Generally, immersion is a form of purification, not sanctification. Usually, but not always. Maimonides adds the phrase "from impurities," but since Exodus 19 does not state that the Israelites were impure, there was no need for purification in this case.[24] This ritual immersion achieved sanctification, not purification. Maimonides emphasizes the point in the *Guide*, where he preserves the phrase, "God commanded [Moses] to sanctify the people." Kornfeld also understands this as "consecrate" (p. 530).

This one verse shows how widely the root *k-d-sh* can be interpreted. Onkelos and Rashi emphasize the element "prepare." Philo, Kimhi, Nahmanides, and Sarna, believe *k-d-sh* here means "purify." Maimonides and Kornfeld understand it as "sanctify."[25]

---

24. This diverges from Kimhi's exegetical comment that the Israelites were impure since they dwelled among an impure people (on Ezek. 16:9).

25. Similar divergences can be multiplied, e.g., Num. 11:18 and 1 Sam. 7:1

Chapter 3

Lexical Analysis II:

The Fourfold Relationship
(*Ḳ-D-SH*, *T-H-R*, *Ḥ-L-L*, and *T-M-'*)

They shall teach my people the difference between the
holy and the profane, and show them how to distinguish
between the unclean and the clean.

— Ezekiel 44:23

This section will examine four Hebrew roots: *ḳ-d-sh* (holy),
t-h-r (pure), *ḥ-l-l* (which can mean "common" or "defiled"),
and *t-m-'* (impure). The relationship of these four terms, and
concomitant concepts, will be explored in this chapter.

Jacob Milgrom writes, "Persons and objects are subject to
four possible states: sacred, common, pure, and impure. Two
of which can exist simultaneously—either sacred or common
and either pure or impure. Nevertheless, one combination is

excluded in the priestly system: whereas the common may be either pure or impure the sacred may not be impure" (1991: 616). The holy is distinct from the common, but is restricted from the impure. A three-point clarification is in order.

First, the holy is restricted always to the impure, sometimes to the common, and in limited cases even to the other sacred objects.

Second, the Hebrew root *ḥ-l-l* has two meanings, "profaneness," and "commonness." In some places, *ḥ-l-l* simply means "ordinary," e.g., "*ḥol* bread" (1 Sam. 21:5), which was neither deficient nor defiled, but still unsatisfactory because David's troops had been "sanctified" for battle. In other places, *ḥ-l-l* is used to indicate a great offense: "They… have profaned [*ḥ-l-l*] My Sabbaths" (Ezek. 23:38). When *ḥ-l-l* is used to mean "desecration," then it is restricted to the holy. However when *ḥ-l-l* means "common, ordinary," then sometimes it is permitted to the holy and other times forbidden.

Third, *t-m-'*, "impure," has two opposites: *k-d-sh*, "holy," and *t-h-r*, "pure." The roots *t-h-r* and *t-m-'* are logically complementary; in the Jewish system it is necessary that every object in the world is either pure or impure. However, we can also speak of distance from the common, which leads to restriction: *t-m-'* is "restricted and inferior," whereas the root *k-d-sh* is "restricted and elevated." To this extent, *k-d-sh* and *t-m-'* are semantic opposites. Milgrom writes, "These two terms represent antonymous and antagonistic realms whose fusion or confusion is potentially lethal" (1994: 556). To this extent, Peterson writes, "Uncleanness and holiness function as something of polar opposites, though not as lexical binary opposites."[26]

These four terms share a unique relationship, which gets to the heart of how holiness and impurity operate, and their relationship reveals the philosophical and theological ramifications of holiness itself.

Multiple Meanings of *Ḥ-L-L*

As a broad term, *ḥ-l-l* is the logical complement of *ḳ-d-sh*; anything not holy is common. In this sense, *ḥ-l-l* is the default status of an object—it is assumed to have no restriction about it, either from holiness or impurity. In a narrow sense, *ḥ-l-l* refers to the misuse of holy objects, whence *ḥ-l-l* is a near synonym of *t-m'*.

Tawil suggests that originally *ḥ-l-l* "in its concrete-physical connotation is clearly employed to mean 'to pierce, to bore a hole,'" and he traces the "semantic development of the root [*ḥ-l-l*] from the physical-concrete meaning 'to pierce through, bore' to its abstract transferred sense, 'to profane'" (2012: 117). The root *ḥ-l-l* in some contexts has semantic overlap with *t-m-'*, "defile," such as: "And that you may put difference [*b-d-l*] between the holy [*ḳodesh*] and the common [*ḥol*], and between the unclean [*tamei*] and the clean [*tahor*]" (Lev. 10:10, cf. Ezek. 44:23).

---

26. Peterson 1984: 79. Gorman also uses the pairings holy/not-holy and pure/not-pure (1990: 220), which demonstrates how these terms are logical complements.

Theories of Impurity

The idea of impurity (*tumah*) is used in several contexts. According to Maimonides, it can refer to three things: religious violations, dirt and/or filth, or ritual defilement (see *Guide* 3:47). The most expansive use of the root *t-m-'* is the ritual concept of purity and impurity, which is also the most foreign to the modern reader. Nonetheless, these concepts are central to the biblical religion, so are worthy of investigation. Furthermore, since impurity is the opposite of holiness, it is necessary to examine the mechanics and theories of impurity. We will look at eight general theories about ritual impurity.

The first theory is that impurity is essentially dirt, and possibly inhabited by demonic forces. This has been quoted in many places, normally by people who reject the theory. In the modern era, which is blessed with scientific knowledge, it is easy to dismiss the equation of dirt with ritual defilement. But if for just a moment we transform to a pre-scientific mindset, it would not be unreasonable for a rational society to conclude that corpses, dead animals, and curious growths were demonically malignant entities (see, e.g., Douglas 2002: x-xi).

However, both Maimonides and Hirsch repudiate the theory that impurity is related to dirt. Maimonides writes, "impurity is not mud or filth that can be washed away with water" (*Mikva'ot* 11:15), and Hirsch calls the theory "absolute folly" (p. 355).

The second theory is that impurity is truly and veritably caused by sin. There is at least one Midrash that suggests that the *hatta't* is brought on account of sin (*be-khol makom ein ha-yahid mevi hatta't ella al het* — *Canticles Rabbah* 5:1). However, this theory appears difficult, since in several places the impurity does not seem to emerge from a sin.

A third theory is that holiness is a form of perfection. Aryeh Kaplan says that holiness is the opposite of death and imperfection. Mary Douglas similarly envisions "the Holy as wholeness and completeness. Much of Leviticus is taken up with stating the physical perfection that is required of things presented in the temple and of persons approaching it" (2002: 63-64). Milgrom even goes so far as saying, "Holiness implies moral as well as ritual perfection" (1991: 696). The inverse is that impurity is something that is, in some rigorous sense, significantly flawed or deficient.

The fourth theory is put rather graphically, "According to their love is their uncleanness, so that no one may turn the bones of his father and mother into spoons" (*Yadayim* 4:6). The Rabbis accepted the rationale that impurity is proportional to its level of affection. Man is the most beloved of all creatures because he was created in the Divine image, which is why the lifeless form of man is the most potent source of impurity. The rationale of the Mishnah itself, "according to their love is their uncleanness," requires investigation. An Israelite corpse generates impurity, since the human form is the most beloved of all earthly creations. It is unclear how the other sources of impurity, like dead rodents, conform to this rationale. It is, of course, possible that this Mishnah is not seeking a comprehensive theory, but a polemical point against the Sadducees' rejection of rabbinic doctrine.

A fifth theory is put forth by Maimonides:

... the object of the Sanctuary was to create in the hearts of those who enter it certain feelings of awe and reverence, in accordance with the command, "You shall revere my sanctuary" (Lev. 19:30). But when we continually see an object, however sublime it may be, our regard for that object will be lessened, and the impression we have received of it will be weakened. Our Sages, considering this fact, said that we should not enter the Temple whenever we liked, and pointed to the words: "Make thy foot rare in the house of thy friend" (Prov. 25:17). For this reason the unclean were not allowed to enter the Sanctuary, although there are so many kinds of uncleanness, that [at a time] only a few people are clean (*Guide* 3:47).[27]

Maimonides explains that the impurities are numerous and divinely installed to ensure that man will not become unimpressed by the most significant and sacred sites and rites.

The sixth theory is from Milgrom, who believes that impurity is closely related to death (1991: 45; see there). Rabbi Joseph Soloveitchik also takes this theory, writing, "Death and holiness constitute two contradictory verses, as it were, and the third harmonizing verse has yet to make its appearance" (1983:36). The possible exceptions are the *metzora* (so-called "leper") and *yoledet* (parturient). The *metzora* can be compared to a dead person, as Moses said when Miriam was afflicted: "Let her not be like a corpse" (Num. 12:14, *Nedarim*

---

27. Maimonides elsewhere refers to the laws of *tumah* as *ḥukkim* (*Mikva'ot* 11:15), which for him are commandments that possess a rationale, though not one that is immediately apparent. Homiletically, he says that these laws are an allusion to developing purity of thought and action (*Mikva'ot* 11:15, *Guide* 3:33).

64b, Milgrom 2000: 1721). The *metzora* also has the same purification ritual as someone who has been in contact with the dead. Nahmanides' theory of impurity is a hybrid, but is related to both death and illness (see his comments on Lev. 15:11).

The seventh theory is presented by Propp, who writes, "Birth and death both represent transitions between nonbeing and being" (2006: 685). Similarly, Gorman writes, "These may be explained on the basis of their concern with the boundaries between life and death and the crossing of these boundaries" (1990: 137 n. 1). This theory is consistent with holiness and impurity as liminal items, as Douglas noted.

Rabbi S.R. Hirsch provides an eighth theory. Hirsch writes, "It is clear that the prototype of impurity is a dead human body. Nothing points more strikingly to human beings having willy-nilly to submit to the forces of Nature's demands" (on Lev. 7:26). He further writes, "impurity is identical with that of lack of freedom of will, and that the laws of impurity are instituted to work against this idea wherever it is likely to be awakened in us by any object of circumstance" (on Lev. 4:11-12: see also on Lev. 11:39-40 and Levy's comment there). To highlight the difference between Milgrom and Hirsch: Milgrom ties impurity to the paradigm of death, while Hirsch suggests that since every living thing will eventually perish, it teaches that freedom of the will has limitations, since life eventually submits to the forces of death.

For Hirsch, the converse is that holiness is the truest expression of freedom of the will: "holiness is nothing but the absolutely free-willed readiness for the fulfillment of the laws of morality given by God" (on Lev. 20:26; see also on Lev. 11:43).

We have just delineated eight theories of impurity: (1 demonic dirt, (2) sin, (3) imperfection, (4) converse or loss of belovedness, (5) prevent overexposure, (6) death, (7) liminal items, and (8) free will and man's inherent limitations.

Bifurcating the Impure and the Holy

Ancient man did not distinguish between the holy and the impure. Both were taboo, and the primitive mind had little concern whether the threat was from one side or the other; the practical danger was of more significance than its source. W.R. Smith writes, "even in the more advanced nations the notions of holiness and uncleanness often touch" (1889: 153). He observes the similarity between the two, "Holy and unclean things have this in common, that in both cases certain restrictions lie in men's use of and contact with them" (p. 446). Milgrom quotes from Kaufmann, "the ancients mainly feared impurity because it was demonic, even metadivine, capable of attacking the gods" (1991: 259).[28]

For example, the Scottish anthropologist Sir James Frazer observes that the Syrians regarded the swine as a sacred beast, but in Hierapolis (in modern-day western Turkey) it was unclean and transmitted impurity; in both cases, it was taboo. Smith provides a different example, "Among the Syrians the

---

28. This should in no way suggest that the Hebrew Bible accepted the theory that impurity was demonic or anything of the sort. There is no biblical evidence to justify just a conclusion. Rather, this type of thinking is likely what the Bible is responding to, by showing that impurity in the Bible is not a capricious concept.

dove was most holy, and he who touched it became taboo for a day" (p. 450). Frazer explains that this perspective "points to a hazy state of religious thought in which the ideas of sanctity and uncleanness are not yet sharply distinguished, both being blent in a sort of vaporous solution to which we give the name of taboo" (pp. 471-472).

However, in the Bible the ideas of holiness and impurity clearly became antonymous literary terms:

> You shall not make yourselves detestable with any swarming thing that swarms, nor shall you make yourselves impure with them, that you should thereby become impure. For I am the Lord your God; therefore sanctify yourselves and be holy; for I am holy; you shall not defile yourselves with any manner of swarming thing that moves upon the earth (Lev. 11:43-44).

Rabbi Judah Halevi, in the *Kuzari*, offers an explanation of the relationship between holiness and impurity:

> Impurity and holiness are contradictory ideas; one cannot be thought of without the other. Without holiness we should not know the signification of impurity. Impurity means that the approach to holy objects, hallowed by God, is forbidden to the person so affected. Such would be priests, their food, clothing, offering, sacrifices, the holy House, etc. In the same way the ideas of holiness include something which

forbids the person connected with it to approach many ordinary objects (*Kuzari* 3:49).[29]

According to the *Kuzari*, holiness and impurity are co-dependent concepts. Holiness requires impurity, and vice versa, in order for the terms to have any meaning at all. Maimonides grounds the *Kuzari*'s statement within the confines of law: "Scripture has cautioned those who are ritually impure against entering the Sanctuary or consuming offerings, *terumah*, or the second tithe. There is, however, no prohibition at all against consuming ordinary foods while impure" (*Tum'at Okhlin* 16:8).

Similarities of Holiness and Impurity

Nonetheless, there are several common factors between holiness and impurity. First, as noted, they seem to have often overlapped in pre-biblical times. Second, they both have the semantic component of "separated." (Holiness is separation by elevation; impurity is separation by degradation or demotion.) Third, they have ritualized elements of restriction about them.

Here we will focus on a fourth similarity: holiness and impurity both have a natural tendency to expand; they are both "contagious." According to Milgrom, holiness and impurity "are dynamic: they seek to extend their influence and control over the other two categories, the common and the pure…."[30] In the most dramatic example, the Mishnah teaches, "uncleanness

---

29. Similarly, Nahmanides writes, "whoever guards himself from impurity shall be called holy" (on Exod. 19:10, quoted above), and Milgrom calls the terms "semantic opposites" (1991: 1002).

30. Milgrom 1991: 732. Gorman calls this quality "dynamic" (1990: 93). The idea of sacred contagion has already been observed in Durkheim (1915: 314-315).

extends upward and extends downward" (*Oholot* 7:1), which demonstrates this dynamic and expansive nature. Holiness, too, has an expansive quality. However, even in these cases, Peterson notes that the holy is not contagious in the same way in which the impure is contagious. Only a very few things may become holy, whereas many more items are open to defilement (1984: 79). The idea of contagious holiness appears five times in the Bible, frequently using a phrase *kol ha-nogea' bah yiḳdash*: the altar (Exod. 29:37), certain sacred vessels (Exod. 30:26-29), the meal offering (Lev. 6:11), and the purification offering (Lev. 6:20). There is also a peculiar case of contagious holiness in the book of Haggai (2:12-14).

The Hebrew word *kol* can be rendered "whoever" or "whatever." Milgrom says that in this verse, *kol* means exclusively *things*, "whatever touches [the altar] will become sanctified," to the exclusion of humans (2000: 1431). The question is also asked if *yiḳdash*, "shall become holy," applies to objects that are "suitable" for sanctification or even unsuitable objects. According to the Talmud, the outer altar only sanctifies what is suitable while the inner altar sanctifies even what is unfit for the altar (*Zevaḥim* 27b, Maimonides, *Pesulei ha-Muḳdashin* 3:18). Rashi explains, based on Exod. 30:26, that the inner altar was anointed with oil, which is why it sanctifies anything, even incense that is not fit for it. Its elevated status means that the inner altar sanctifies objects, so to speak, even against their will.

The fifth case of contagious holiness is from the book of Haggai. Where the first four cases deal with specific rituals, the final case has a more polemical flavor:

"If a man carries holy flesh in the fold of his garment, and with this fold should touch bread, stew, wine, oil, or any food, shall it be holy [*ha-yikdash*]?" And the priests answered and said, "No." Then Haggai said, "If one who is defiled by a dead body touches any of these, shall it be impure [*ha-yitma*]?" And the priests answered and said, "It shall be impure" (Hag. 2:12-13).

There is clearly a polemical component to this passage. Haggai is less concerned with the priests' answers to the technical questions, since he immediately issues a condemnation. Hildebrand even raises the possibility that Haggai was asking about ethical holiness all along (p. 163). It is also possible that Haggai was using the question to transition from familiarity with ritual to ethical human decency. Haggai tested the priests' knowledge and simultaneously condemned their character, reminding them that impurity spreads more easily that holiness.[31]

Impurity and Sin

On a biblical level, impurity is not caused by sin, and it is not sinful to remain in an impure state. Maimonides writes, "whoever desires to remain in his state of impurity and not enter the camp of the Divine Presence is permitted to do so" (*ShM*, Pos. 109). Nahmanides also records that the Rabbis commanded

31. Plato notes a similar ideal requirements for a priest, "first, as to whether he is sound of body and of legitimate birth; and in the second place, in order to show that he is of a perfectly pure family, not stained with homicide or any similar impiety in his own person, and also that his father and mother have led a similar unstained life" (*Laws* 6:729). According to Plato, both proper lineage and proper conduct are necessary for priesthood.

that people purify themselves before festivals (on Lev. 11:8, quoting *Rosh Hashanah* 16b), which implies that there is not otherwise an obligation. Milgrom is emphatic that "contracting impurity is no sin! ... The sin rests only in his neglect to purify himself of his impurity... within the prescribed one-day time limit... thereby increasing the possibility that he will pollute the sanctuary and its sancta" (1991: 298). Perhaps the Sages decreed across-the-board purification during the festivals because when everyone makes the pilgrimage to Jerusalem, there is a greater concern of impurity spreading.

The *Ḥinnukh*, though accepting that there is no biblical prohibition to remain impure, concludes, "Nonetheless, the early pietists and men of great deeds did not have the habit of remaining defiled, because impurity is disgusting and purity is beloved, and a person's soul is elevated and refined by purity" (*Ḥinnukh* 175). Even though the *Ḥinnukh* accepts Maimonides' ruling on a halakhic level, he advocates a higher ideal.

Chapter 4

Lexical Analysis III:
Words of Elevation and Degradation

*Man has discovered something that is separate
from the world, but he does not know what it is.*

— Rabbi Joseph Soloveitchik[32]

In both the Tanakh as well as subsequent literature, the
root *ḳ-d-sh* is used with many words that imply separation.
However holiness is not merely to be understood as separation
from the undesirable. The root *ḳ-d-sh* is used in many literary
contexts with other roots of additional forms of elevation or
degradation, and those usages enhance or reveal additional
shades of meaning.

Ḳ-D-SH and Glory (*K-B-D*)
In at least four places the root *ḳ-d-sh* is used with the root *k-b-d*,
"glory, honor, respect":

---

32. 2008: 23.

- And there I shall meet the children of Israel to be sanctified [*k-d-sh*] in My glory [*k-b-d*] (Exod. 29:43-44).

- And Moses said to Aaron: This is what the Lord spoke, saying: By those close to me I will be sanctified [*k-d-sh*], and in front of the entire people I will be honored [*k-b-d*]... (Lev. 10:3).

- Holy, holy, holy is the Lord of hosts; the whole world is filled with His glory [*k-b-d*] (Isa. 6:3).

- And say: Thus declares the Lord God: Behold, I am against you, O Zidon, and I will be glorified [*k-b-d*] in your midst, and they shall know that I am the Lord, when I shall have executed judgments against her, and I shall be sanctified [*k-d-sh*] in her (Ezek. 28:22).

Aster has noted that both are common descriptions for God, and he writes, "Generally, God's name is prasied as distinct from those of more mundane beings," using words like *k-d-sh*, "holy" (Isa. 57:15) and *k-b-d* (Deut. 28:58; Aster 2012: 159 n. 76). Gammie points out that "glory" is called "holiness uncovered" (1989: 86-87 n. 35). This might be consistent with the verse, "Show me Your glory" (Exod. 33:20), which Maimonides says refers to "the essence, the reality of God" (*Guide* 1:64).

Peretz Segal, however, argues *k-d-sh* and *k-b-d* "are used as synonyms for divine retribution" (p. 91), i.e., the wrath of God, based on Lev. 10:3 and Ezek 28:22. However, I am not convinced that Segal is correct, since Exod. 29:43-44 and Isa. 6:3 (above) also use the pair without any immediate mention of wrath. Rather, the pairing *k-d-sh* and *k-b-d* indicates God's immediately observable manifestation or action. In some cases, that manifestation will be in the form of punishment, but not necessarily.

Ḳ-D-SH and Greatness (G-D-L)

The words ḳ-d-sh and g-d-l appear at least twice:

- Thus will I magnify [g-d-l] Myself, and sanctify [ḳ-d-sh] Myself, and I will make Myself known in the eyes of many nations; and they shall know that I am the Lord (Ezek. 38:23).
- Let them praise Your great [g-d-l] and awesome [nora] name; it is holy (Ps. 99:3).

The first verse is the source for the Ḳaddish prayer, which contains many other terms for praise and elevation. When the terms "holiness" and "greatness" are juxtaposed, it evokes a specific emotion and psychological recognition and acknowledgement from those who encounter His greatness.

Ḳ-D-SH and Blessing (B-R-Ḳ)

The root ḳ-d-sh also appears with b-r-k, "bless." As an aside, it should be noted that the English word "bless" has changed its meaning. According to the OED, "The etymological meaning was… 'to mark (or affect in some way) with blood (or sacrifice); to consecrate.'" However, in contemporary speech, the English word "to bless" is distinguishable from "to sanctify, consecrate," and the focus in this chapter is on the Semitic roots related to b-r-k, not their English-language counterparts.

The terms *k-d-sh* and *b-r-k* are used together in Tanakh in the following instances:

- And God blessed [*b-r-k*] the seventh day and sanctified [*k-d-sh*] it, because on it He rested from all His work which God had created to make (Gen. 2:3).
- Look down from Your holy habitation, from heaven, and bless Your people Israel (Deut. 26:15).
- The Lord bless you, O abode of righteousness, O holy hill! (Jer. 31:22).
- Bless the Lord, O my soul, and all that is within me, bless His holy name (Ps. 103:1).
- Lift up your hands *k-d-sh* and bless the Lord (Ps. 134:2).[33]
- … all flesh will bless his holy name for ever and ever (Ps. 145:21).

Genesis 2:3 is the first place that either "sanctify" (*k-d-sh*) or "bless" (*b-r-k*) is used. Rashi writes that *b-r-k* is a bountiful concept, but *k-d-sh* is restrictive: "'And he blessed [*b-r-k*] it' with the manna; every day, bread descended for them in their proper amounts, but on the sixth day a double-portion [descended]. 'And He sanctified it,' that the manna did not descend at all on the Sabbath." Here, *b-r-k* is consistent with the standard rabbinic interpretation of "additional goodness" (based on *Genesis Rabbah* 11:9). For Rashi, *k-d-sh* means that the manna would not fall, based on the future prohibitions of gathering and carrying on the Sabbath. Thus for Rashi,

---

33. The grammar of this verse makes it difficult to know if it should be rendered "Lift up your hands *in holiness*" or "towards the Temple" (Radak).

"blessing" and "sanctification" in this verse are working at cross purposes. It is not just wordplay to say that the Sabbath's holiness, according to this Midrash, overrides its blessedness.[34]

Many commentaries disagree with Rashi's distinction between "sanctified" and "blessed." First of all, in the Midrash, Rabbi Nathan states: *berkho ba-man ve-ḳiddesho bi-verakhah,* "He blessed it with the manna and sanctified it with the blessing."[35] In other words, according to Rabbi Nathan, the sanctification *comes through* blessing. Nahmanides also points out that Rashi does not provide the simple reading of the verse; rather, Rashi's Midrash illustrates the restrictive nature of the Sabbath after the Torah was given. Philo of Alexandria takes it even further: "closely akin are the character that is charged with benediction and the character that is holy" (*Allegorical Interpretations* I.7[17]).

The Sages have interpreted "blessedness" as an additional benefit. Hence blessedness in this verse is a material description. Holiness, however, is not a material description; thus God's final act of creation was to create metaphysics, to create that which lies beyond the physical. Specifically, He created the metaphysical idea of sanctity. Holiness is the fulcrum from the end of the creation to the beginning of the rest of world.

Ḳ-D-SH and Elevation

The root *ḳ-d-sh* is also used with many words meaning "elevated" in the sense of exaltation, including *addir* ("majestic"), *nora,*

---

34. Ibn Ezra and *Akedat Yitzḥak* also see a restrictive meaning of *ḳ-d-sh* in this verse (see Harvey 1977: 12-13).

35. The commentary *Etz Yosef* says this refers to the "blessing" over the wine [presumably of Friday night].

(from *y-r-'*, "awesome, revered"), *rum* ("elevated"), and *nissa* ("uplifted"):

- Who is like you, O Lord, among the gods? Who is like you, majestic in holiness [*ne'dar ba-kodesh*], awesome in splendor [*nora tehillot*], doing wonders? (Exod. 15:11),
- Let them praise Your great [*g-d-l*] and awesome [*nora*] name; it is holy (Ps. 99:3),
- Holy and awesome [*nora*] is His name (Ps. 111:9),
- The name of the great [*gadol*], mighty [*gibbor*], revered [*nora*], God and King, holy is He (introduction to the *Shema*),
- … in Your holy, great [*gadol*], and revered [*nora*] we trust" (introduction to *Shema*),
- Extol [*romemu*] the Lord our God; worship at his footstool; Holy is he (Ps. 99:5),
- Extol [*romemu*] the Lord our God, and worship at his holy mountain; for the Lord our God is holy (Ps. 99:9).
- For thus says the high and lofty [*ram ve-nissa*] one who inhabits eternity, whose name is Holy: I dwell in the high and holy place [*marom ve-kadosh*], and also with those who are contrite and humble in spirit, to revive the spirit of the humble, and to revive the heart of the contrite (Isa. 57:15). This verse, on which the introduction to *Shokhen Ad* is based, uses several different terms for elevation.

It is also worth noting that Even-Shoshan's primary definition of *kadosh* is *na'aleh ve-nisgav*, which are two words for "elevated." Aster also observes a thematic connection between the words *kadosh, nora, nikhbad,* and *addir* in describing God's name (2012: 159 n.76).

Ḳ-D-SH and Wholeness (*SH-L-M*)

Holiness is related to that which is whole, complete, or perfect. In fact, it has been suggested that "holy" is etymologically related "whole," as the *Oxford English Dictionary* writes:

> It is with some probability assumed to have been "inviolate, inviolable, that must be preserved *whole* or intact, that cannot be injured with impunity".... But it might also start from *hail-* in the sense of "health, food, luck, well-being," or be connected wih the sense "good omen, auspice, augury."

Conceptually, Mary Douglas similarly understands "the Holy as wholeness and completeness. Much of Leviticus is taken up with stating the physical perfection that is required of things presented in the temple and of persons approaching it" (2002: 63-64). Inversely, Gorman believes defilement is a "disruption of proper order (wholeness)" (1990: 224-225).

Tawil raises a similar possibility, writing, "Consequently, though unattested the root *h-l-l* 'to pierce, bore' seems to serve as an antonym of the root *sh-l-m* 'whole' i.e., free from damage or defect."[36] Hence, holiness seems very closely related to completeness and perfection. There is no verse that uses *k-d-sh* and *sh-l-m* consecutively, but there is a significant retinue

---

36. Tawil 2012:118-9. The Hebrew characters have been transliterated.

of commentators that sees holiness as thematically (if not linguistically) related to wholeness.[37]

Ḳ-D-SH and Knowledge

Holiness is predicated on knowledge. It is not sufficient to say that God sanctifies Israel; the knowledge of this fact is stressed: "You must speak to the children of Israel and say, 'You must surely keep my Sabbaths, because it is a sign between Me and you for all generations to know [la-da'at] that I am the Lord who sanctifies you'" (Exod. 31:13).[38] There is also the curious phrase da'at ḳedoshim, which appears twice in Proverbs (9:10, 30:3).

Philo of Alexandria also recognized knowledge as a precondition of holiness: "When the soul of the virtuous man becomes filled with the contemplation of wisdom, which, like the day and the sun, *illumines the whole reason and the mind*, then it begins to give birth to opposites in the separation of distinction and discrimination *between holy and profane*." (*Questions and Answers on Genesis* IV.158; emphasis added).

Maimonides writes, regarding the dietary laws:

> It is a positive commandment to know [leida] the signs
> that separate [a permitted from a permissible animal],

37. There is also a ritual relationship between ḳ-d-sh and sh-l-m, as Onkelos consistently translates zevaḥ shelamim as nikhsat ḳudshayya (e.g., Lev. 3:1).

38. It is unclear here *who* is supposed to have this cognition. The Talmud understands that God tells Moses He wishes to inform Israel about the gift of the Sabbath (*Shabbat* 10b, *Betzah* 16a). Saadiah understands it in the second person, "that you [plural] shall know." Finally, Rashi and Maimonides (*Guide* 3:26) say "to know" refers to the other nations of the world, in the third person.

whether a domesticated animal, wild animal, bird, fish, or locust, that are permitted to eat from those that are not permitted to eat (*Ma'akhalot Asurot* 1:1).

Maimonides writes that there is a specific commandment merely to know the signs. In this case, knowing (*yedi'ah*) facilitates separation (*havdalah*) between pure and impure animals, which allows ritual purity (*taharah*), which ultimately paves the way for holiness (*kedushah*).

The relationship between knowledge and holiness also appears in the liturgy. The Saturday night prayer includes *havdalah* in the blessing *Attah honen* (i.e., in the blessing of "knowledge," following the opinion of Rabbi Joseph at *Berakhot* 33a): "You have favored us with *knowledge* of your Torah, and taught us to perform the laws of your will. You have *separated*, Lord our God, between the *holy* and the *common* ...." R. Jonah of Gerona comments, "and [we recite] *havdalah* in *honen ha-da'at* because through *knowledge* we recognize the greatness of rest, and *we know how to distinguish between the holy and the common*" (*Rif* 23b, s.v. *ve-havdalah*).

Ḳ-D-SH and Anointing (*M-SH-Ḥ*)

In two verses, the concepts holiness and anointing (*meshihah*) are used together:

- And every day you shall bring a bull as a purgation [*hatta't*] offering, for atonement [*k-p-r*], and you shall cleanse [*h-t-'*] the altar when you atone [*k-p-r*] for it, and you shall anoint [*m-sh-ḥ*] it to sanctify [*k-d-sh*] it (Exod. 29:36).

- On the day when Moses had finished setting up the tabernacle and had anointed [*m-sh-ḥ*] and sanctified [*ḳ-d-sh*] it and all its vessels and had anointed [*m-sh-ḥ*] and sanctified [*ḳ-d-sh*] the altar with all its vessels (Num. 7:1).

However, the text does not identify the specific relationship between "anointing" (*meshiḥah*), and "sanctification." The Talmud understands the sequence *m-sh-ḥ... ḳ-d-sh* as one continuous process, referring to oil specifically (*Shevuot* 15a; Maimonides, *Klei ha-Miḳdash* 1:12; Nahmanides on Num. 7:1). Thus the verse, "and he anointed it *and* consecrated it" (Num. 7:1) has the same meaning as, "and he anointed it *to* consecrate it" (Exod. 29:36).

Ibn Ezra, however, views anointing (*meshiḥah*) and sanctifying as two distinct rituals, "'and anointed' with the anointing oil, 'and sanctified' with blood." Ibn Ezra draws a parallel from the priests and their garments to the tabernacle and its vessels: just as the priests and the sacerdotal garments are sanctified with blood, the tabernacle and its vessels are also sanctified with blood (Exod. 29:21; where Ibn Ezra says blood has a purifying property).

Nahmanides responds to Ibn Ezra and defends the talmudic understanding, writing, "the tabernacle was never sanctified with blood, rather Moses anointed them in order to sanctify them." Baruch Levine, following this talmudic reading, marshals evidence from the ancient Near East that anointing with oil alone was often sufficient to achieve sanctification, "When oil was poured on objects, such as altars and stelae, it served to consecrate them as well" (2006: 254).

K̲-D-SH and *N-Z-R*

The root *n-z-r* is worth examining because the *nazir* (Numbers 6) is generally considered one of the paradigms of holiness. There is a debate whether the root *n-z-r* originally bore a sacred meaning or only acquired it by extension:

- Non-sacral origin: Rashi takes a very generic view that *n-z-r* always means *perishut* (on Lev. 22:1, Num. 6:2, Isa. 1:4), which has to be understood as any separation—elevation, demotion, or neutral corresponding to Menahem b. Saruk's three categories—because the context there is separation *from* God. Even-Shoshan defines *n-z-r* as "separated [*b-d-l*] and distinct [*p-r-sh*]." Jastrow also gives a primary meaning of *n-z-r*, "to surround; to keep off; to set apart." Milgrom writes, "*n-z-r* means 'separate oneself.' And if the separation is for God then it implies sanctification" (1990: 44). Levine writes, "Both roots, *n-d-r*, which is attested in Ugaritc and Phoenician, and *n-z-r*, are probably phonetic variants of the same verbal root, which is posited as **n-d̲-r*, on the bases of the Arabic cognate *nad̲ara*" (1993: 2119).
- Sacral origin: W.R. Smith writes, "the Arabic *nadhara* and the Hebrew נזר both mean primarily 'to consecrate'" (1889: 482). *BDB* renders it, "dedicate, consecrate," or "separate, in relig. and ceremonial sense."

The root *n-z-r*, however, is frequently (but not exclusively) used to mean separation by elevation:

- the priest wears a *nēzer*, "diadem," on his head (Exod. 29:6),

- Samson is given the title *nezir Elohim*, "the separated one to the Lord" (Judges 13).
- the Temple officials are called *n-z-r*, "her *n-z-r*'s were purer than snow" (Lam. 4:7); the word has been variously translated as "princes," "consecrated ones," "dignitaries," and "nobles."
- a Nazirite, one with unshorn hair, perhaps as an ornamental representation of hair or the head.[39]

Thus even though the majority opinion is that *n-z-r* was a generic word for "separation" (like *b-d-l* and *p-r-sh*), it commonly came to be used in sacred contexts.

Ḳ-D-SH and Ḥ-R-M

The Hebrew root *ḥ-r-m* also has an original idea of generic separation. In Akkadian, *ḫarāmu* means "to separate," and the *CAD* provides the example: *ḫarāmu ša parāsu*, "for the sake of separating." Even-Shoshan records that *ḥ-r-m* can mean both "destroy" and "sanctify," and that the noun *ḥērem* can mean "something sanctified to God (or a priest)," or "something of forbidden use." Consider the following two passages:

- Surely no *ḥ-r-m* that a man makes *ḥ-r-m* to the Lord from whatever he owns—from man, beast, or field

---

39. Hair is a liminal item, since it stands at the border of the body and the outside world, so one would expect its treatment to be regulated, in accordance with the theory put forth by Mary Douglas. W.R. Smith noted that the Arab pilgrim "cannot cut or dress his hair" (1889: 481), while Greeks would "offer the hair on deliverance from urgent danger" (1889: 332), and that "some Semitic priests let their hair grow unpolled, like Samuel, and that others kept it close shaved, like the priests of Egypt" (1889: 483).

of his inheritance—it shall not be sold and it shall not be redeemed. Anything *h-r-m* is holy of holies to the Lord (Lev. 27:28).

- And surely guard yourselves from the *h-r-m* lest you violate the *h-r-m* if you take from the *h-r-m* and make the camp *h-r-m* and cause trouble in it. But all silver, gold, and vessels of brass and iron are holy [*k-d-sh*] to the Lord, and they shall come to the treasury of the Lord (Josh. 6:18-19).

Milgrom makes the distinction between "war-*ḥērem*" and "peace-*ḥērem*" (2001: 2392). In both cases, *h-r-m* is juxtaposed with *k-d-sh*. In the first passage, *h-r-m* is defined as "most holy," whereas in the second instance *h-r-m* is antonymous with *k-d-sh*. Hence the root *h-r-m* had an original idea of separation, and grew in two directions, one negative (e.g., Josh. 6:18-19), and one positive (e.g., Lev. 27:28). The negative *ḥerem* can never be desacralized (i.e., it is "super holy" and not subject to redemption). The positive *ḥerem* is divided into two groups: priestly *ḥerem* belongs to the priests forever, while Temple *ḥerem* is designed to be auctioned off (redeemed), and the funds used to maintain the Temple.

K-D-SH and Desanctification (P-D-H and G-'-L)

Hebrew has a special idea of removing the sanctity—sometimes removing its *ḥerem*—of an object, represented by either *p-d-h* or *g-'-l*. The *BDB* defines *p-d-h* as "ransom," but in some contexts may be better translated as "redeem." The *BDB* translates *g-'-l* as "redeem," specifying "by payment of value assessed, of consecrated things, by the original owner."

Specifically, in the context of redeeming the firstborn, the roots *ḳ-d-sh* and *p-d-h* are used in close proximity (Exod. 13:2, 13; Num. 18:15-17). In Exodus 13, man is obligated to sanctify "whatever opens the womb," but that statement is limited to allow for the firstborn of humans and donkeys to be redeemed. In Numbers, the firstborn of bulls, sheep, and goats cannot be redeemed because they are holy. Since these bulls, sheep, and goats are permitted on the altar, they carry a higher level of sanctity than the other species, even man, in this regard.

Another Hebrew word for "redeem" is *g-'-l*, and is often used to describe a kinsman who acts as the "redeemer of blood" (Num. 35:19). The word *g-'-l* can also refer to redeeming property that was dedicated to the sanctuary (Leviticus 27), as well as homiletically, "And they shall call them the holy nation, the redeemed ones [*g-'-l*] of the Lord" (Isa. 62:12).

Ḳ-D-SH and Hierosylia (M-'-L)

The Hebrew root *m-'-l* is used antonymously with *ḳ-d-sh*.[40] It is difficult to ascertain the exact meaning of *m-'-l*, but the key passage is, "Whoever commits *m-'-l* and sins unknowingly against the holy objects of God [*mi-ḳodshei YHVH*] shall bring his reparation offering to the Lord..." (Lev. 5:14-15). *M-'-l* has been defined as "act unfaithfully, treacherously" (*BDB*), "sacrilege" (Milgrom 1991: 320), or "trespass" (Deut. 32:51, KJV), and designates misuse of holy objects (Lev. 5:14), or against *ḥerem* (Josh. 7:1).

The previous section analyzed how holiness can be safely and systematically removed from an object using the word

---

40. For a full development of *m-'-l*, see Milgrom 1991: 345-356.

g-'-l. On the other hand, *m-'-l* is the consequence of misuse without proper desanctification.

The roots *k-d-sh* and *m-'-l* are also contrasted metaphorically in the following verse:

> Because you trespassed [*m-'-l*] against Me in the midst of the children of Israel at the waters of Meribath-kadesh, in the wilderness of Zin; because you did not sanctify [*k-d-sh*] Me in the midst of the children of Israel (Deut. 32:51).

Here the use is clearly metaphorical rather than legal, but the consequences are no less severe, since this event (according to many authorities) is what precluded Moses from entering Israel.

Ḳ-D-SH and Profligacy (*Z-N-H*)

Another root to consider is *z-n-h*, "commit adultery," but it is used metaphorically in relation to holiness, e.g., "and you shall not stray after your hearts or after your eyes which you lust [*z-n-h*] after. So that you will remember and perform all My commandments, and you shall be holy [*k-d-sh*] to your God" (Num. 15:39-40).

The root *z-n-h* appears again in the apocryphal book of Jubilees. When Reuben cohabited with Bilhah, his father's concubine, Jacob responded, "And there is no greater sin on earth than the adultery [*z-n-h*] which they have committed, because Israel is a nation holy [*k-d-sh*] to God..." (Jub.

33:20).[41] The use of *z-n-h* in Numbers is metaphorical, while its appearance in Jubilees is more literal; yet both are contrasted with holiness. Furthermore, there may be a parallel between sacrilege (*m-'-l*) and *z-n-h*: Sacrilege designates the misuse of sanctuary property, where *z-n-h* is used for inappropriate sexual contact (see also Deut. 23:18.19).

Holiness and Lack of Circumcision ('-R-L)

According to Rashi, the root *'-r-l* means *atum*, "blocked, clogged" (on Jer. 6:10), and refers to, among onther things, the state of being uncircumcised. [42] Due to that negative connotation, the root *'-r-l* is frequently used as a synonym for *t-m-'*, and in that capacity it is used antonymously with *k-d-sh*, e.g, in agricultural laws:

> When you enter the land and plant any kind of fruit tree, you shall regard its fruit as forbidden [*'-r-l*, twice]. For three years it shall be forbidden [*'-r-l*] to you; it shall not be eaten. And in the fourth year, it shall be a holy offering of praise to the Lord (Lev. 19:23-24).

The Rabbis say that fruit that grows in the first three years may not be eaten or used at all (*Bava Kamma* 101a; Maimonides, *Ma'akhlot Asurot* 10:9). The agricultural laws of Lev. 19:23-24 should be compared to the livestock laws of Exodus 13. Arboreal growth—fruit from trees—is *'-r-l*. The firstborn of

---

41. Cf. Gen. 49:4, which uses *ḥ-l-l*, "defile." Notice the semantic development *ḥ-l-l* → *z-n-h*.

42. Propp notes that Arabs called circumcision *taharah*, "purification," thus pairing the roots *'-r-l* and *t-h-r* (236).

73

man and donkey must be redeemed (*p-d-h*), the firstborn of permissible animals must be sanctified (*ḳ-d-sh*), but the first fruits of trees are '-*r-l*, "forbidden, uncircumcised."

Isaiah uses '-*r-l* with *t-m-'* and *ḳ-d-sh* regarding geographic restriction:

> Arise, arise, and gird your strength, O Zion, your garments of splendor, O Jerusalem, city of the Temple [*ḳ-d-sh*], because the uncircumcised ['-*r-l*] and impure [*t-m-'*] shall not continue to pass through you (Isa. 52:1; cf. Ezek. 44:9).

Isaiah is presenting an extreme example, where the holiness will be so powerful that it excludes the uncircumcised and the impure. The relationship between '-*r-l* and *t-m-'* also appears regarding one's lips. Moses says that he cannot speak to Pharaoh because he is of "uncircumcised ['-*r-l*] lips" (Exod. 6:12), whereas Isaiah says, "I am a man of unclean [*t-m-'*] lips" (Isa. 6:5). Thus '-*r-l* is used fundamentally to describe a state of deficiency. In halakhic matters, this deficiency is often symbolized as a lack of pruning arboreal growths or lack of circumcision in humans. In rhetorical contexts, '-*r-l* is used for any deficiency, as opposed to the idea of wholeness or perfection.

Holiness as a "Positive Concept"

Even though holiness carries with it a partial definition of separateness, the Hebrew root *ḳ-d-sh* is highly correlated with other positive ideas, such as honor, elevation, and blessedness; and negatively correlated with terms of degradation such as impurity (*tumah*), *zenut*, and *ḥerem*. The prior analysis should demonstrate that holiness is what Milgrom called a "positive concept" (1991: 731).

Linguistic analysis corroborates this point, by comparing the frequency of two phrases, *ḳ-d-sh l-* ("holy to") and *ḳ-d-sh m-* ("holy from"). The phrase "holy to" is much more prevalent, for example: "Sanctify to Me every firstborn" (Exod. 13:2; cf. Deut. 15:19), "a Sabbath day holy to the Lord" (Exod. 16:23, cf. Exod. 20:8, 31:14-15; 35:2), and "you shall be a holy people to Me" (Exod. 22:20).[43] Thus holiness demonstrates a positive aspect of possession, ownership, or control, for a specific, but somehow desirable purpose. Alternatively, the use of *ḳ-d-sh m-* ("holy from") to signify removal and withdrawal is much rarer.[44]

W.R. Smith noted that holiness "often brings special taboos with it" (1889: 425). Smith suggests that holiness is primarily defined by the taboos or restrictions that holiness entails. This is only half of the equation, since holiness also has an affirmative value. Abraham Joshua Heschel noted, "Its negativity and separateness is but a protective screen for the positive aspect of the sacred" (1965: 48). Clines weaves Smith's idea of taboo with Milgrom's statement that holiness is a positive concept: something holy is "regarded as belonging to the deity, in a positive sense resulting in need for removal from ordinary use or pollution, or need for special treatment" (*DCH*, p. 190).

43. A non-exhaustive list includes: Exod. 28:3; Exod. 28:36; Exod. 30:10; Exod. 30:32; Lev. 19:24; Lev. 21:7; Lev. 23:7; Lev. 23:20; Lev. 27:14; Lev. 27:30; Num. 3:13; Num. 6:8; Num. 15:40; Num. 28:7; Deut. 7:6; Deut. 26:19; Josh. 6:19; Judg. 17:3; 2 Sam. 8:11; 1 Kings 9:7; 2 Kings 10:20; Jer. 2:3; Ezek. 45:4; Ezek. 45:6; Ezek. 48:14; Zech. 14:20-21; Ezra 8:28; Neh. 8:9; 2 Chron. 35:3.
44. Some examples are Lev. 16:19; 2 Sam. 11:4; 2 Sam. 8:11.

Anthropologically, Durkheim makes the same observation. In one place he writes, "By definition, sacred beings are separated beings" (1915: 377), but later writes, "our definition of the sacred is that it is something added to and above the real..." (469). To call something holy is not just to say it is withdrawn from common or secular use; it is to assert that since some person, object, or place is removed from secular use, it engages in a relationship with the Divine.

Chapter 5

Holiness of God and Man

"And who can say of himself 'I am holy.'"

— Father Païssy, *The Brothers Karamazov*

The root *k̲-d-sh* is often used as a name or attribute of a deity. E. Jan Wilson notes that as early as the third millennium BCE, some of the gods were called "holy," but cautions, "Although one might expect the gods to be called holy, that does not occur with any great frequency" (1994: 30). In Ugarit, the word *k̲-d-sh* is used simply as a name for a god: "In some of the literary texts from Ugarit, the term *qdš* is used as a divine epithet. The gods are sometimes called 'the sons of *qdš*,' in the parallelism 'the gods // the sons of *qdš*'" (Van Koppen 1999: 415). It also seems that there were multiple gods known by some form of the root *k̲-d-sh*.

In the Hebrew Bible, when *k̲adosh* appears a noun, it sometimes refers to God. For example, "To whom shall you compare Me and who shall I be compared to, says Kadosh" (Isa. 40:25), This verse emphasizes at once His holiness and incomparability (see also Isa. 57:15, Hab. 3:3, and Job 6:10). Isaiah also repeatedly refers to God as "the Holy One of Israel," and this terminology is also preserved in the common rabbinic term for God, "the Holy One, Blessed is He." Based on this, it is reasonable to conclude that anything that is called "holy" possesses a special relationship with God. This is a powerful, if obvious, conclusion, because it asserts that whatever his holy is related to the divine. J.L. Mays, clearly beholden to Otto, writes, "'Holy' is a synonym for God; it indicates the numinous and dynamic, the *mysterium tremendum*, the incomparable awesome force of the divine" (1969: 158).

Furthermore, it seems that the root *k-d-sh* is used primarily to describe the gods—and not to describe mortals—in ancient Near Eastern literature. In the Yehimilk Inscription, likely dating from the tenth century BCE, the gods are called holy, but not man. Similarly, the Eshmunazar Sarcophagus uses the root *k-d-sh* three times, and all seem to refer to the holiness of the gods, not man. In Ugaritic, there were several classes of priests, including *khnm* and *qdšm*, but little is known of the role of these classes except their names.[45] Biblical priests are similarly called holy (*k-d-sh*), and even actively sanctified by both God and man. Krahmalkov, in his dictionary of Phoenician and Punic, defines *k-d-sh* as an adjective, "holy," but only quotes places where it refers to deities (and once to a queen), but never to ordinary people (2000: 425-426). Similarly, the *Dictionary of North-West Semitic Inscriptions* provides numerous examples of calling the

---

45. Pardee writes, "From the ritual texts themselves, we know of a *qdš*, 'holy person,' whose role it is to sing, but we know nothing about what other roles the persons played who belonged to this category" (Pardee 2002: 239).

gods holy. But in four and a half pages of citations, that dictionary offers only one single example of *ḳ-d-sh* used in reference to people, and that is from an inscription from Beth Shearim, which is well into the Common Era. "These are the sarcophagi, the inner and the outer / are of Rabbi Aniana and of ... / the holy ones [= *ha-ḳedoshim*], the sons of ...." Avigad writes, "This is the first time that this designation [i.e., *ha-ḳedoshim*], attributed to human beings, appears in Hebrew epigraphy. Evidently it should be interpreted as holy, saintly men, in the sense of righteous, pure or chaste..." (1957: 241-242).

This research gives the impression that in the ancient Near East, the attribute of holiness was applied primarily to deities, not humans. The concept of lay-holiness may have been absent at this point. All of this stands in sharp distinction to one of the biblical models of holiness, which calls on everyone to be holy: "speak to the *entire assembly* of Israel and say to them: Be holy, because I the Lord your God am holy" (Lev. 19:2). In other words, one of the key biblical developments was to provide a more expansive definition of holiness that could apply to the laity as well as the priesthood.

Sanctification of God (in Torah, Prophets, and *Halakhah*)

There are several places in the Bible where God's sanctity is displayed. In Pentateuchal sources, God's being sanctified is a public display. This public display is either performed by God Himself, or by others, but there is a clear theme throughout the early biblical books.

For example, "speak to the *entire assembly* of Israel and say to them: Be holy, because I the Lord your God am holy"

79

(Lev. 19:2). The verse could have merely said, "speak to Israel," but adding the words "entire assembly" demonstrates the expansive nature of this message, and according to one rabbinic tradition this was spoken at *ḥakhel* when the entire congregation, including men, women, and children, would have been present. In this verse, God declares Himself holy before the entire nation, and says the Israelites will also be holy. Several other verses that demonstrate the public nature of sanctification:

- "And there I will meet with the children of Israel, and [the tabernacle] will be sanctified by My glory" (Exod. 29:43). In this case, God's presence will "meet" with the entire nation of Israel.
- "By those close to Me I will be sanctified and before the entire nation I will be honored" (Lev. 10:3).
- "And you shall not profane My holy name, and I will be sanctified among the children of Israel" (Lev. 22:32).
- "Because you did not have trust in Me, to sanctify Me in the eyes of the children of Israel, therefore you will not bring this congregation into the land which I have given them. This is water of Meribah; because the children of Israel contended with the Lord, and He was sanctified in them" (Num. 20:12-13; the public nature of this event is recorded again in Num. 27:14 and Deut. 32:51).

The previous section showed the root *ḵ-d-sh* is often used as a name for the gods in the ancient Near East and perhaps the Bible as well. This section takes it further, that it is not just a name or even a description, but God's sanctification is fundamentally displayed and manifested in a public setting.

Snaith sees a shift of God's sanctification in the times of the eighth-century BCE prophets, especially Isaiah, who states that God is *nikdash bi-tzedakah*, "sanctified by righteousness" (Isa. 5:16). So when Isaiah said, "sanctified by righteousness," Snaith observes a clear divergence from holiness as a grand observable event (yet one without an obvious moral claim) to holiness being manifest through righteousness. This conclusion is definitely possible, based on the ethical orientation of the prophets Isaiah, Hosea, and Amos.

God's sanctification has another development in the book of Ezekiel, approximately a century and a half after Isaiah. Ezekiel's doctrine of sanctification is similar to the earlier biblical books, but has two significant additions. First, sometimes the sanctification is for Israel, while sometimes it is for the heathen nations; in the Pentateuch, the sanctification is always for the sight of Israel. Second, the sanctification is often used with the verb *y-d-'* ("know") that God has done this:

- "I will be glorified [*k-b-d*] in your midst, and they will know that I am the Lord, when I will have executed judgments against her, and I shall be sanctified in her" (Ezek. 28:22).
- "When I will have gathered the house of Israel from the people among whom they are scattered and I will be sanctified in them to the eyes of the nations, then they will dwell in their land that I have given to My servant Jacob" (Ezek. 28:25, cf. Ezek. 39:27). In this verse, the public display seems specifically for the gentile nations.

- "And I will sanctify My great name which has been profaned among the nations, which you have defiled among them, and the nations will know that I am the Lord, declares the Lord God, when I am sanctified in you before their eyes" (Ezek. 36:23). This verse refers to God's sanctification twice, and both times before the heathen nations. It refers to God's decision, which in context is unilateral and unprompted by repentance, to publicly redeem the Israelites (v. 24), purify them (vv. 25-29), and give agricultural abundance (v. 30), so the nations will know what God has done (v. 36).[46]

Ezekiel was a priest, yet his doctrine of holiness—especially his doctrine of sanctification of God—is remarkably universal, since it primarily involves knowledge among the nations, rather than isolated among a small cohort of religious functionaries.

In rabbinic times, an idea arose of "sanctification of the Name" (*kiddush Hashem*). Rav Adda bar Ahavah, a second-century (CE) Amora, rules that all matters of holiness require a *minyan*, based on the verse, "I will be sanctified among the children of Israel" (*Berakhot* 21b). Later, R. Hiyya bar Abba (third-fourth century) applied the same verse and logic to other public matters. The Talmud remains faithful to the biblical

---

46. Other verses that continue this theme are, "that the nations will know Me when I am sanctified in you before them" (Ezek. 38:16), "I will make Myself great and I will be sanctified, and I will be known in the eyes of the many nations" (Ezek. 38:23), "And My holy Name I will make known in the midst of My nation Israel" (Ezek. 39:7), "When I have brought them again from the nations and I have gathered them from their enemies' lands and I will be sanctified in them before the eyes of the many nations" (Ezek. 39:27).

notion that God is sanctified in the public realm. The only difference is that in biblical times, public sanctification meant theophany, while in talmudic times, it meant a public ritual, but in both cases the central point is the public element.

Martyrdom

Biblical Hebrew possesses no term for "martyrdom," but in rabbinic terminology, it is *kiddush Hashem*, literally, "sanctification of the Name." The English word "martyr" comes from the Greek *martus*, "witness." The same linguistic phenomenon exists in Akkadian, Ugaritic, and Arabic; those languages all use the same word for "martyr" and "witness." Rabbinic terminology is unique in Semitic languages in using "sanctification of the Name" for "martyrdom."

In Biblical Hebrew, the phrase "sanctification of the Name" appears five times. Three of those five regard Moses' striking the rock in the wilderness of Zin:

- And the Lord spoke to Moses, saying: Since you did not believe in Me to sanctify Me in the eyes of the Children of Israel, therefore you will not bring this congregation to the land that I have given you (Num. 20:12).
- Because you have rebelled in the wilderness of Zin, in the strife of the congregation, to sanctify Me at the water, before their eyes, which is Meribath-kadesh in the wilderness of Zin (Num. 27:14).
- Because you trespassed against Me in the midst of the children of Israel at the waters of Meribath-kadesh, in the wilderness of Zin; because you did not sanctify Me in the midst of the children of Israel (Deut. 32:51).

The final two are in different contexts:

- When he sees his children, the work of My hands, in the midst of him, that they sanctify My name, they shall sanctify the Holy One of Jacob, and shall stand in awe of the God of Israel (Isa. 29:23).
- And I shall sanctify My great name, which has been profaned among the nations, which you have profaned in their midst, and the nations shall know that I am the Lord, declares the Lord God, when I shall be sanctified through you before their eyes (Ezek. 36:23).

Moses' transgression at Zin is considered a failure to sanctify God's name, but there is not even a hint of martyrdom in these verses.

Many commentaries derive the commandment to martyrdom from, "And you shall not profane My holy Name, and I shall be sanctified among the children of Israel; I am the Lord who sanctifies you" (Lev. 22:32). The Bible contains no shortage of characters willing to die for their faith. Isaac let himself be bound on Moriah, Jephtah's daughter did not protest being brought as a sacrifice for her father's victory, Samson slew the Philistines though he thereby ended his own life, and Saul loathed death at the hands of the Philistines as the most ignominious end, but no biblical passage uses *k-d-sh* regarding their deaths.

Conceptually, the willingness to be martyred originates from the third chapter of Daniel. Three steadfast and stalwart men, Shadrach, Meshach, and Abed-Nego, were thrust into the fiery furnace, and they emerged unharmed. (In other words, they were willing to die, but ultimately survived; and the root *k-d-sh* appears nowhere.) Another possible source is the Scroll of the Hasmoneans (i.e., *Megillat Antiochus*), which contains the line, "it is better for us to die in a cave than to violate [*h-l-l*] the Sabbath" (Birnbaum 1977: 719).

Ultimately, the use of *k-d-sh* to describe martyrdom is firmly talmudic. No other Semitic language uses *k-d-sh* regarding martyrdom, and the combination of *k-d-sh* with martyrdom never appears in the Bible, despite the numerous characters willing to die for their faith. However, it is not surprising, because in the Bible, the Divine Name is sanctified through public acts by either God or man, and there is ostensibly no more public act than the willingness to perish for one's devout beliefs.

Holiness of Persons

There are different degrees of holiness, but according to Judaism, all human life possesses inherent sanctity. According to Malbim, mankind is *kadosh*, which he defines as *muvdal ve-na'aleh min ha-teva u-moshel aleha*, "separated and elevated from nature, over which he rules." Rabbi Hirsch presents the idea of human holiness differently: "the whole Torah rests primarily on making the body holy. The whole mortality of human beings rests on the fact that the human body with all its urges, forces, and organs, was formed commensurately with the Godly calling of Man, and is to be kept holy and dedicated exclusively to the Godly calling."

Holiness is also applied to the Israelites, as it says: "And the Lord spoke to Moses saying: Speak to the entire congregation of Israelites and say to them, 'You shall be holy, because I the Lord your God am holy'" (Lev. 19:2). The Midrash explains, "You shall be holy…" [Lev. 19:2]. Can you be as holy as Me? This comes to teach [that you should be holy] *because* I am holy. [However], My holiness is greater than your holiness" (*Leviticus Rabbah* 24:9). We have already seen that holiness applied to individuals is only present in the Bible but not elsewhere in the ancient Near East.

The Levites are an intermediate case; although they have certain privileges not available to a regular Israelite, the Torah does not say they are "sanctified." Rather, God takes (*l-ḳ-ḥ*) them (Num. 3:12-13), separates (*b-d-l*) them (Deut. 8:10), and Moses purifies (*t-h-r*) them (Num. 8:5-7). Milgrom concludes this is a conscious description, writing, "in matters of holiness they rank no higher than the laity" (1990: 64, 1991: 519). Furthermore, the Levites are substitutes for the firstborn, who are called holy.[47] Nonetheless the Levites are called "holy" later in the Bible (2 Chron. 23:6, 35:3), and many later authorities ascribed holiness to the Levites. For example, Ibn Ezra and Nahmanides say the "holy ones" of Deut. 33:3 refers to the Levites, and Malbim is also willing to ascribe holiness to the Levites (on 1 Sam. 1:11).

The next level is the priests. The priests are also commanded to holiness, and the language is shockingly similar to that of the Israelites: The Israelites are commanded, "You shall be holy, because I the Lord your God am holy" (Lev. 19:2). Priests: "They shall be holy to the Lord their

---

47. There is also a theory that the Levites are *not* initially called holy because that would recall that the firstborn were involved in the sin of the Golden Calf.

God" (Lev. 21:6). The difference is a legal one. The narrative explains that priestly holiness is higher than Israelite holiness because they are forbidden to defile themselves to non-familial dead and to enter into certain forbidden marriages (Lev. 21:7).[48] Only priests may offer incense (Num. 17:5; cf. 2 Chron. 26:18). Although the priests have many additional restrictions, they also have additional privileges. They are the only ones permitted to consume the most holy offerings (the ones that are not fully incinerated), and they are accorded the twenty-four gifts of priesthood. This is another manifestation of holiness as a positive concept: the priests, by virture of their enhanced holiness, are privileged to the flesh of the higher-level offerings as well as other gifts that are associated exclusively with the priesthood.

The highest level of personal holiness belongs to the High Priest, of whom God states, "I am the Lord who sanctifies him" (Lev. 21:15). He is further restricted from defiling himself even on account of his relatives, from departing the Sanctuary to tend to the needs of a dead relative, and from marrying any woman save a virgin (Lev. 21:11-14). He is also the only person responsible for performing the service on the Day of Atonement—a fusion of spatial, temporal, and personal holiness.

Until now we have seen a funneling of holiness from man (Malbim, Hirsch), the Israelites (Lev. 19:2), the Levites (an

---

48. Van der Toorn suggests the prohibition of the priests defiling themselves to the dead is primarily an Israelite one: "The Mesopotamian texts hardly refer to the defilment incurred by the contact with a human corpse. The ideal of a swift and proper burial of the dead is apparently owing more to a concern for the welfare of the ghosts (*eṭemmu*) of the deceased than to a fear of contamination" (1985: 37).

intermediate case), the priests (Lev. 21:6), and the High Priest (Lev. 21:15). Besides them, there are certain anomalous cases, the most famous of which is the Nazirite, who is not permittied to drink wine, cut his hair, or defile himself to the dead (Num. 6:1-21). The Nazirite voluntarily assumes the restrictions and the status of the High Priest, and while that comparison is not made explicit in Scripture, the Midrash makes the connection: "The Holy One, blessed be He, said, behold he is as important as the High Priest. Just as the High Priest is forbidden to defile himself to any corpse, a Nazirite is also forbidden to defile himself to any corpse" (*Numbers Rabbah* 10:11). Neither the officiating priests nor the Nazirite may consume wine.

Both Milgrom and Shamah draw a connection between the Nazirite's unshorn hair and the High Priest's head that is anointed with oil (Lev. 21:12; Milgrom 1991: 357; Shamah p. 710).

Verse 5 reads: "All the days of his vow of Naziriteship no razor shall come on his head; until the days be fulfilled that he vows to the Lord, shall be holy, he shall let the locks of the hair of his head grow long." In the original Hebrew, it is ambiguous what the phrase *kodesh yihyeh* refers to. Rashi says that the Nazirite's hair is the referent here, since it cannot shorn. Seforno disagrees and believes the phrase refers to the Nazirite himself. Either way, the hair must be burned after his term is completed, because the hair retains its holy character after the Nazir himself has been desanctified.[49]

49. Hizkuni on Num. 6:16, s.v. *tahat*. Milgrom 1991: 420-421.

The Nazirite undertakes the prohibitions that are normally associated with the High Priest. The Nazirite oath requires the individual to conduct his life in an elevated level of holiness. The High Priest's precinct of service is, paradigmatically, the innermost chamber of the Temple. The Nazirite has the exact same restrictions, even though he has no additional privileges of office in the Temple or of bringing and partaking of any additional sacrifices, since genetically he is not a priest.

There are two ways to understand this phenomenon. First, it may be suggested that the Nazirite, like the High Priest, should be removed from the outside world. He cannot interact with the rest of society, lest he imbibe strong drink or defile himself to the dead; furthermore, since he has become a recluse, he has no need to maintain his appearance. He may let his hair grow long and he will not be shamed, since he lives a life of seclusion and isolation. An alternative approach is that the Nazirite's precinct is the entire world. Although the Nazirite has additional restrictions, those prohibitions teach him how to engage the world and navigate it properly in the face of numerous obstacles and temptations. Once a Nazirite has successfully endured a certain amount of time (after all, a violation of the Nazirite oath resets the count to zero), he can then depart from this status. He cannot shed the status of Naziriteship until he has succeeded in his new, higher state. Once he has learned to operate in the world with the severest restrictions, he should have little difficulty maintaining the ordinary level of holiness that is expected of an average Israelite.

The Nazirite has an additional unique feature. He can be desacralized. In this way, he is closer to redeemed sanctuary property than a human being. However, the text never uses *p-d-h* or *g-'-l*, two words which are used of property.

Elisha

Elisha's holiness is one of the most peculiar mentions of personal holiness in the Bible: "And she said to her husband, 'Behold now, I see that this is a holy man of God that passes by us continually'" (2 Kings 4:9). Joshua Berman has noted that Elisha is the only individual explicitly called holy, and he observes, "this term is used neither by God, nor by a prophet, nor even by the biblical narrator, but merely by a minor character within the story, [which] serves only to highlight the exceptional nature of this usage" (1995: 4). The text does not mention what makes Elisha holy, but there seem to be several basic approaches:

1. The Targum and Joseph Kara say this holiness is because Elisha is a man of God. (Hebrew *ish*, "man," but also used to mean "prophet").
2. According to one opinion in the Talmud, Elisha is called holy because the Shunnamite woman never saw a fly pass by his table (one opinion at *Berakhot* 10b). The Mishnah says that in the Temple, miraculously, no fly was ever seen despite the presence of raw meat (*Avot* 5:5). The Maharsha (Rabbi Samuel Eidels) understands that Elisha's "table was holy, like the altar, of which it is said, 'and no fly was seen in the slaughterhouse.'" (s.v. *she-lo*). The Talmud elsewhere equates the altar with the household table (*Menaḥot* 97a). Therefore, according to this opinion, the holiness of Elisha's table was akin to the holiness of the altar.

3. The Shunnamite woman spread a sheet of linen over his bed, and she never saw a nocturnal emission on it (the second opinion at *Berakhot* 10b). Rashi however presents the two talmudic explanations as one unified answer.

4. Gersonides suggests that Elisha comported himself in such a way that his holiness was recognized. This approach downplays the role of miracles and identifies holiness with a refined character. Nonetheless, Gersonides does not identify which behaviors allowed the Shunmmite woman to detect that Elisha was holy.

5. He was a miracle-worker, which is explicit in the narrative. This may also be what Omanson intended in writing, "In this context the concept of holiness does not refer primarily to moral goodness but rather to power that comes from being close to God" (2008: 769; this opinion is diametrically opposed to that of Gersonides). However, the text does not call Elisha holy *because* of this ability.

6. Gray writes that Elisha was "ritually sacrosanct, [which] made it unsafe for the Shunammite couple to entertain him in their common premises, hence an upper chamber was to be built for him" (1971: 495). Gray is probably building on the notion of holiness as a contagion, discussed earlier. However, Jones persuasively rejects Gray, writing, "Other evidence from the *OT* to confirm that contact with the prophets was avoided is not produced, and it would seem more reasonable to suggest that she simply wished to offer permanent and comfortable hospitality arrangements for the prophet because of her belief that he would bring a blessing to her house" (1984: 404-405).

There are thus at least six ways that Elisha's unique holiness is understood: (1) miracle-worker, (2) prophet of God, (3) high moral character, (4) contagion, (5) free from flies, or (6) free from seminal emissions.

Korah

Korah said to Moses and Aaron, "You take too much upon you, seeing the entire congregation is holy, every one of them, and the Lord is among them; why then do you lift up yourselves above the assembly of the Lord?" (Num. 16:3). The Midrash relates the famous parable that Korah asked if a garment that is entirely blue still requires fringes on the corners. He complained, "A garment that is entirely blue does not exempt it, but the four blue threads exempt it." Again he moaned, "A house filled with holy books does not exempt a doorpost of a *mezuzah*, but one section of the Torah exempts it." Korah therefore concluded that Moses was making these laws up on his own. R. Bahya b. Asher offers the following explanation: "Korah used the example of the house full of sacred texts and the cloak of blue wool as a parable of the Jewish people. He meant that since the Jewish people are all holy, there is no need to appoint a High Priest to perform the function for the people which the fringes performed for the cloak."

Korah did not object to degrees of holiness of places, seasons, or other objects. It was restricted to degrees of difference between people. This is why he midrashically concluded, "you are inventing them on your own." The verse in Lev. 19:2 is a command to holiness that applies to all of Israel, and Lev. 21:6 is a uniquely priestly holiness. Both exist in the Bible, and both must be reckoned with. Thus Rabbi Soloveitchik writes, "The cry of Korah and his followers... is partly true and partly false. It is correct that the external, exoteric holiness of the community of Israel, which obligates all of us to perform the commandments, does not distinguish between great and small. However, internal, esoteric holiness is dependent on the greatness, breadth, and depth of the individual" (2008: 59).

Chapter 6

Holiness of Place, Time, and Objects

The holiness of places is one of the key concepts in understanding holiness in general. Mircea Eliade provides an anthropological explanation of the difference between sacred space and neutral space:

> For religious man, space is not homogeneous; he experiences interruptions, breaks in it; some parts of space are qualitatively different from others.... There is, then, sacred space, and hence a strong, significant space; there are other spaces that are not sacred and so are without structure or consistency, amorphous....
> no break qualitatively differentiates the various parts of the mass (1959: 20-22).

Eliade's idea of "strong, significant space" can be contrasted with what Jean-Paul Sartre wrote in *Nausea*: "Nothing happens while you live. The scenery changes, people come in and go out, that's all. There are no beginnings. Days are tacked on to days without rhyme or reason, an interminable, monotonous addition." The antidote to this interminable monotony is distinction in both time and space.

Two biblical examples conform to Eliade's theory, and they contrast "strong" space with "amorphous" space. The first is the scapegoat on Yom Kippur, "and he shall send the he-goat to the desert" (Lev. 16:22). A second example is the purification of the *metzora*, of whom it says, "he shall send the living bird to the open field" (Lev. 14:7). In these two cases, the he-goat and the living bird are sent to an "amorphous" region—an area other than its significant point of origin. Gorman simply refers to this as a "place of chaos" (1990:73), which is contrasted with structured, ordered space representing the holy.

Indicators of Holy Space

The most common form of marking spatial holiness is immurement (surrounding the area with walls). However, sometimes there is not always a physical barrier that exists between rings of spatial holiness. In these cases, the holiness of space must be indicated in another way, and we will explore two alternatives: removing of one's shoes (discalceation), and walking or marching around an area (circumambulation).

Discalceation

The most famous example of discalceation is where God commanded Moses to remove his shoes beside the burning bush because he was standing on holy ground (Exod. 3:5). Joshua had a similar episode, although this was from a messenger of God, not God Himself (Josh. 5:15). Here, the holiness of the land mandates discalceation, even though the reader is never cued about the transition from common to holy ground. The reader is not told if the change is sudden or gradual, and how far the radius of holiness extends.[50]

Why was Moses bidden to remove his shoes? First, Milgrom writes that "sandals, being fashioned of animal skins, are eo ipso impure, but only in regard to the sacred" (1991: 654). Milgrom's thesis, however, has an anachronistic tone to it, since it presupposes an idea of impurity even before the Sinaitic theophany.[51]

Second, Sarna says discalceation is a sign of respect: "the sandals accumulated dust and dirt, and were therefore removed before entering the house. For the same reason, it was not considered proper or respectful to come into a sacred place without first casting off one's footgear."[52] Cassuto also writes, "do not tread on this ground with your travel-soiled sandals." Similarly, priests in the Temple almost certainly did not wear shoes. There certainly is evidence that Moses had a priestly function, or at least a priest-making function in the Bible, which

---

50. This is reminiscent of Wordsworth's lines, "Where holy ground begins, unhallowed ends, / Is marked by no distinguishable line." See "A Parsonage in Oxfordshire" (1820), ll. 1-2.

51. It is possible that cultures in Egypt and Midian had their own systems of impurity, which might resurrect Milgrom's argument, but then one would be forced to argue that God would command Moses to observe a pagan notion of impurity before Sinai, which is a stretch.

52. Sarna 1986: 39-40. See also Propp 1999: 200. In a somewhat similar vein, Rabbi Joseph B. Soloveitchik writes, "The shoe is the symbol of vulgarity and uncouthness, of superficiality, of raw power: 'upon Edom I cast my shoe' (Ps. 60:10). To understand holiness, to gain sensitivity, a person must 'remove his shoes'" (quoted in *Chumash Mesoras Ha-Rav* p. 24).

would explain why Moses is commanded to act in a sacerdotal and reverential role.

Third, Rabbi S.R. Hirsch writes, "Taking off one's shoes expresses giving oneself up entirely to the meaning of a place, to let your personality get its standing and take up its position entirely and directly on it without any intermediary." Similarly Kornfeld says, "the removal of sandals represents a renunciation of any claims to possession" (p. 529). Roland de Vaux, without quoting this verse, sets up the inverse idea: "The shoe seems to have served as a probative instrument in transfers of land" (1961: 169), operative in levirate marriage, where the surviving brother's decalceation is a public renouncement of marriage; de Vaux also extends it to possible metaphoric uses (Amos 2:6, 8:6, Ps. 60:10, Sir. 46:19). Walking—especially with shoes—is a form of taking possession, yet man cannot take ownership of the place of a theophany, so he must remove his shoes, since those places exclusively belong to God. This theory harmonizes nicely, as well, with the opinion that the priests in the Temple did not wear shoes.

Friedrich Nietzsche, in *Beyond Good and Evil*, writes, "there are holy experiences before which they have to take off their shoes and keep away their unclean hands—this is almost their greatest advance toward humanity" (§ 263). The Austrian does not refer to this present verse, even though that section does make reference to "the Bible" in general. For Nietzsche, the ability to create distinctions is a uniquely human and evolved trait; religion would make a congruous argument that the ability to distinguish items is the beginning of the path to holiness. The element of discernment is embedded in the narrative of creation as well, where the root *b-d-l*, "to separate," is used five times (Gen. 1:4, 6, 7, 14, 18). Now that Moses is about to commence a mission that will begin the world afresh by bringing the Torah from heaven to earth, Moses too was instructed to learn the difference between holy and profane. Since Moses was to lead the nation from the amorphous mentality of slavery to the elevated status of freedom, Moses himself was tested to see if he was willing to accept the distinctions that religion frequently demands.

A fifth and final answer, and the most mystical one, can be quoted from Nahmanides, who writes that the places became holy when the *Shekhinah* (Divine Presence) descended upon it: "the entire mount was sanctified when the *Shekhinah* descended upon the top of the mount, just like when the Torah was given… And the Sages said, 'Wherever the *Shekhinah* is revealed, it is forbidden to wear shoes.'" Perhaps this is why the Temple priests were not permitted to wear shoes—the *Shekhinah* was there as well.

Despite these answers, one rabbinic passage views this revelation to teach the opposition effect: "A certain gentile once asked Rabbi Joshua b. Korhah, 'Why did the Holy One, blessed be He, see fit to speak to Moses from a burning bush?' … [He answered:] To teach you that there is no place devoid of the Divine Presence, even a bush." This Midrash reflects a desacralization of space. Moses was bidden to decalceate because he was standing on ground holier than other places; however, the Midrash emphasizes not the holiness of the ground, but the possibility of God being manifest anywhere.

Circumambulation

A second indicator of spatial holiness is circumambulation. This concept appears in ancient Near East texts: "then with Pisangunuqu at the head, Papsukkal, Nusku, and Sha(?) shall proceed, circling the temple" (*ANET* 338-339). It also appears in the Bible, for example when Joshua commanded his men— and the priests with the ark specifically—to circumambulate Jericho seven times for seven days (Joshua 6). The sacral component is clear, not just from the presence of the priests and the ark, but also because Joshua warns the army from partaking of the *ḥerem*, since that will be dedicated to God. Another example is when the city of Jerusalem is rededicated and purified (Neh. 12:27-43).

The act of circumambulation is common in world religions. In Islam, those making the *hajj* to Mecca are expected to circumambulate the Kaaba, the holiest site of that faith, in a ritual known as Tawaf. Worshippers are supposed to circumambulate that site seven times, three times briskly and four times deliberately. Similarly, Hindus and Buddhists perform an act of Parikrama, a circumambulatory action that precedes or is part of prayer. Thus a symbolic act of circling a specific area can also designate or indicate its sanctity.

Sinai, the Tabernacle & the Temple

There are three significant places whose blueprint is described in detail. They are Mount Sinai during Divine revelation, the Tabernacle in the wilderness, and the Temple in Jerusalem. The inauguration of the Tabernacle described in Leviticus 9 uses much of the same imagery and language as the theophany at

Sinai (Exodus 19). Milgrom, following Nahmanides, writes that this overlapping vocabulary "renders the Tabernacle the equivalent of Mount Sinai" and explains that the Tabernacle "becomes a portable Sinai" (1991: 574). It will be instructive to see the relationships between the respective zones of the Sinai, the Tabernacle, and the Temple.

The lowest level of the Sinai is the foot of the mountain, where Moses built an altar and twelve pillars (Exod. 24:4), a sort of immurement. Aaron's sons and the seventy elders were permitted entrance to the second level (Exod. 24:1). This level corresponds to the Holy Place in the Tabernacle, where only the priests were granted access, but from which the Israelites were excluded (e.g., Leviticus 7). The third level of Sinai is where Moses ascended but the rest of the nation was excluded, even Aaron and the elders (Exod. 19:20, 34:2). At Sinai, Moses served as the High Priest, and only he was permitted access to the summit. The precipice of Sinai is congruent to the Holy of Holies in the Tabernacle, where only the High Priest may enter (Lev. 16:2). According to this alignment, the foot of Sinai corresponds to the outer part of the Tabernacle, the next level of Sinai to the Holy Place of the Tabernacle, and the summit of the mount to the Holy of Holies.

Joshua had attained an intermediate status, higher than an elder, but lower than Moses. Joshua departs with Moses from the elders, "And Moses got up [with] Joshua" (Exod. 24:13), but did not ascend the mount, "And Moses ascended the mount" (Exod. 24:15), to the exclusion of Joshua. Milgrom believes Joshua was probably left at "the cloud perimeter" in v. 17 (1991: 143). This points to four, not three, levels: the

Israelites collectively, the elders, Joshua, and Moses; each one representing four distinctive levels of holiness.

Gradations of Spatial Holiness

The Mishnah records ascending levels of holiness of locations within the land of Israel, and each ground has increasingly strict laws that define its holiness:

There are ten levels of holiness. The land of Israel is holier than any other lands. And what is its holiness? In that from it they may bring the *Omer*, the first-fruits, and the two loaves, which may not be brought from any other lands. The walled cities [of the Land of Israel] are holier than that, since lepers are sent out of them, and a corpse can be carried within it as long as they desire, but once the corpse is removed, it may not be brought back in. Within the walls [of Jerusalem] is holier than that, since there they eat the lesser holy offerings and the second tithe. The Temple Mount is holier than that, since no man or woman who has flux, nor a menstruant nor parturient may enter there. The Rampart [*heil*] is holier than that, since Gentiles and those defiled by the dead may not enter there. The Courtyard of Women is holier than that, since one who has immersed himself on that day [but is awaiting nightfall] may not enter, but if he enters, he need not bring a purification offering. The Courtyard of Israelites is holier than that, since one who is lacking atonement [one who has immersed and awaited nightfall, but has not brought an offering] may not enter there, and if he enters accidentally, he is required to bring a purification-offering. The Courtyard of Priests is holier than that, since no Israelite may enter except as needed: to rest his hands on an animal he designates as an offering, to slaughter the sacrifice, or to wave the offering. Between the Hall and the Altar [ben ha-ulam ve-la-mizbeah] is holier than that, because nobody who has a blemish or whose hair is not maintained may enter there. The Sanctuary [hekhal] is holier than that, because nobody may enter there without washing his hands and feet. The Holy of Holies is holier than that, because only the High Priest may enter on Yom Kippur during Temple service (Kelim 1:6-9).

This Mishnah claims there are ten levels but lists eleven. Several resolutions have been suggested to this discrepancy. First, Maimonides, in his Commentary, suggests this Mishnah is according to Rabbi Yosi, who believed that the area between the Hall and the Altar [ben ha-ulam ve-la-mizbeah] has the same holiness as the Sanctuary; and that the Sages in fact count eleven. This conclusion would require that the opening statement is the opinion of Rabbi Yosi, and the list of eleven levels represents the Sages' opinion.

R. Hai Gaon believes this Mishnah is according to the Sages. R. Hai notes that the first level is the land of Israel itself, and anyone—Jew and Gentile, priest and layman, the pure and impure—may enter the land of Israel. However, the last ten levels have restrictions about who can enter them, based on tribal affiliation, gender, or state of impurity. Hence only the last ten levels are called "levels of holiness." If R. Hai is correct, then only a place with severe limitations about who can enter is called holy. Alternatively, holiness is not just based on restriction, but on the commandments in general. Since there are certain commandments that can only be fulfilled in Israel (*mitzvot teluyot ba-aretz*), Israel is considered holier than other lands.[53]

Maimonides in the *Mishneh Torah* appears to have taken a different approach:

Mishnah (*Kelim* 1:6-9)	*Transition*	Maimonides (*Bet ha-Beḥirah* 7:12-22)
There are ten levels of holiness.		The entire land of Israel is holier than all the other lands.
The land of Israel is holier than any other lands.		There are ten levels of holiness, one higher than the next.
The walled cities are holier than that		Walled cities are holier than the rest of the land.

The Mishnah says, "there are ten levels of holiness," and commences the list with the holiness of the Land of Israel, which creates eleven items on the list. Maimonides, to resolve the problem, begins by saying the Land of Israel is holier than all other lands, and only afterward introduces the ten levels of holiness, a resolution which satisfies the problem of eleven-that-is-ten, which is also in consonance with the opinion of R. Hai Gaon.

---

53. Rabbi J. David Bleich, in personal communication, takes the approach that the holiness described in this mishnaic passage is directly tied to the increasing level of commandments applicable in Israel.

From a biblical perspective, the term "holy land" is used first at the burning bush (Exod. 3:5), and the angel of God uses it with Joshua (Josh. 5:15). None of these cases refer to the holiness of the land of Israel. Jacob uses the word *nora*, "awesome, revered," (from *y-r-'*) to describe the place where he had his dream (Gen. 28:17), which Rashi says is the place of the holy Temple. The *Kuzari* goes even further: "Do you not see that Jacob ascribed the vision which he saw, not to the purity of his soul, nor to his belief, nor to true integrity, but to the place, as it is said, 'How awesome is this place'" (*Kuzari* 2:14).

A few other points about some of the levels counted in this Mishnah:

- *Holiness of the Land of Israel* — The Mishnah, followed by Maimonides, indicates that the holiness of the land of Israel is legal, since they quote "Wherein lies its holiness? In that from it they may bring the *Omer*, the first-fruits, and the two loaves." There are many other commandments dependent on the land (*mitzvot ha-teluyot ba-aretz*).

  On the other hand, it is commonly assumed that R. Judah Halevi took the ontological approach, saying that Israel was desirable from the beginning of creation, that it is ontologically different, a place inherently revered, uniquely fit for prophecy, and worthy to be called the "gates of Heaven" (2:14). Nahmanides also took this approach; for him the land was too sensitive to suffer sins of a sexual or idolatrous nature (see on Lev. 18:25). David Novak writes that in the opinion of Nahmanides, "The sanctity of the Land of Israel stems from the fact that it is the earthly place where the connection with the transcendant reality of the world-to-come is most proximate" (1992: 92). This is also the opinion of Rabbi Soloveitchik: "The concept of holiness is rooted in the attachment between man and God within the framework of real life. According to the Halakhah, the holiness of certain places and times is identical with the influence of the *Shekhinah* in the here-and-now. The Land of Israel is holy because the *Shekhinah* and prophecy are found there" (2008: 84).[54]

- *Walled Cities* — The other entries on the list are concentric, each zone getting progressively smaller, more restrictive, and holier. The walled cities, however, are an anomaly and rupture this model of concentricity, since there were walled cities throughout the land of Israel. Furthermore, even though the Mishnah says that being free from lepers is a level of holiness, Rashi says this is called purity (on Lev. 10:14; though the Sages said this verse referred exclusively to Jerusalem). Freedom from the impurity of lepers can be called either "holy" (Mishnah) or "pure" (Rashi), demonstrating some fluidity between the terms.

- *Jerusalem* — The Mishnah cites the reason because one eats the lesser holy offerings and the second tithes there. Isaiah also calls Jerusalem a holy city because the uncircumcised and unclean shall no longer enter (Isa. 52:1), regardless of the *ḳodashim kalim* and second tithe. According to Maimonides, there is a difference between the holiness of Jerusalem before it was destroyed, and the Jerusalem that was rebuilt. He writes:

---

54. As will be seen in short order, Maimonides does say that the *Shekhinah* reposes on Jerusalem and the Temple (but not necessarily on the entire Land of Israel).

And why do I say that the first sanctification of Jerusalem and the Temple was eternal, while the holiness of the rest of the land—regarding the sabbatical years and tithes—is not eternal? Because the holiness of Jerusalem and the Temple is from the Divine Presence, and that Presence is never nullified. It is written, "And I shall destroy your sanctuaries" (Lev. 26:31), but the Sages said even though they are destroyed, the sanctity endures.

However, the geographical obligation of the sabbatical year and tithes is only because of a national conquest [*kibbush rabbim*], and since the land has been taken from their hands, that conquest was annulled. And according to the Torah, it became exempt from tithes and the sabbatical year, because it is no longer considered "Israel."

When Ezra came up and sanctified it [again], he did not sanctify it by conquest, but by taking it [*hazakah*]. And therefore, wherever the immigrants from Babylonia took with the second sanctification of Ezra, it is sanctified [even] today and is obligated in the sabbatical year and tithes (*Bet ha-Behirah* 6:16).

Rabbi Joseph Karo, in his gloss on Maimonides, writes, "I do not understand why *hazakah* should be stronger than *kibbush*, or why the *hazakah* should not be annulled when the land was taken from us [the second time]."

Maimonides may have based his ruling on R. Elazar's opinion in the following Midrash:

R. Samuel b. Nahman said: Before the Temple was destroyed, the Divine Presence dwelled within it, as it says, "The Lord is in His holy sanctuary" (Ps. 11:4). When the Temple was destroyed, the Divine Presence was removed to Heaven, as it says, "The Lord in Heaven prepares His throne" (Ps. 103:19). Rabbi Elazar says the Divine Presence has never moved from the sanctuary, as it says, "My eyes and My heart shall be there forever" (2 Chron. 7:16).... And even though it was destroyed, its sanctity endures (*Exodus Rabbah* 2:2).

The sanctity of Jerusalem and the Temple endured because of the presence of the *Shekhinah*, while the first sanctification of the land of Israel was not eternal, while the second one—through settlement, not conquest—was unending. Rabbi Soloveitchik explained similarly: the first inhabitation was on account of military conquest and could be abrogated by military conquest, while the second inhabitation was on account of the Jews engaging in Torah study, which is eternal.[55]

- *The Rampart (ḥeil)* — There is debate if this level of holiness is biblical or rabbinic. Maimonides in his *Commentary* uses the phrase "the Sages said," indicating its rabbinic status. However, in his codification he makes no such indication (*Bet ha-Beḥirah* 7:16). Rabbi Abraham b. David (Raavad) and Rabbi David b. Avi Zimrah (Radvaz) believe it is rabbinic, while Rabbi Joseph Korkus argues it is biblical.

---

55. I heard this quoted from Rabbi Michael Taubes, Rosh Yeshiva of Yeshiva University.

- *Courtyard of Women* — It is only by rabbinic enactment that one who has immersed himself on that day [but is still awaiting nightfall] may not enter.

- *Between the Hall and the Altar (bein ha-ulam ve-la-mizbeaḥ — Joel 2:17)* — The prohibition from blemish is rooted in the Bible: "However he shall not enter through the veil, and he shall not approach the altar, because there is a blemish upon him, and he shall not profane My holy objects,[56] for I am the Lord who sanctifies them" (Lev. 21:23).

  Despite the biblical roots, there is debate about the status of this level. Rav Acha bar Ahavah believes this level is biblical, based on a *gezeirah shavah* (*Yoma* 44b).[57] Rava, dissenting, argues that the level *ben ha-ulam ve-la-mizbeaḥ* is biblical. Since the Talmud leaves this matter unresolved, the debate perpetuates in later sources. Maimonides believes that this level is biblical (at least, according to most of his interpreters), while Raavad and R. Obadiah Bartenura believe this is a rabbinic decree.

- *The Sanctuary [hekhal]* — The *hekhal* required sanctification of hands and feet before entering. Milgrom quotes an ancient Near Eastern parallel that in Mesopotamia, the "*bārû* priest (diviner) prays 'while purifying his mouth and hands with water'" (1991: 960). The washing of hands and feet are prescribed before Temple service, "And Aaron and his sons shall wash [*ve-raḥatzu*] their hands and feet from

---

56. The Hebrew word is plural *miḳdashai*; since "My temples" does not work in context, it is understood as "My holy objects."
57. A rabbinic tool of halakhic exegesis to understand the relationship of two appearances of the same word, which ascribes the legal details of one attestation to the second attestation as well. By its nature, it can only work on a biblical, not rabbinic, level.

[the vessel, *kiyyor*]" (Exod. 30:19). Onkelos translates *ve-raḥatzu*, "and they shall wash" and *vi-ḳaddeshun*, "and they shall sanctify." Nonetheless, Kehati quotes that Raavad and Bartenura consider this level of rabbinic origin.

- *Holy of Holies* — In Egypt, the temples had a different arrangement. Frankfort quotes that in Egypt, for each new temple that was built, "the Holy of Holies of each temple was equally sacred... for, when a new temple was founded, it was assumed that the potential sacredness of the site became manifest" (1946: 21). The Hebrew model clearly rejected such a notion, and shifts from noncentric holiness to concentric holiness.

- *The Ark* — The holiness of the ark is not mentioned in this Mishnah but is also regarded as holy (it was probably omitted from the Mishnah because there are no legal ramifications of who may enter). Sarna says that the ark "constituted the under-structure of the sacred space above it, space that was imbued with the extra-holiness radiated by the Divine Presence" (1986: 211). The Psalm describes God as *yoshev keruvim*, "dwelling between the cherubim" (Ps. 99:1; cf. Exod. 25:22), about which the *The Complete ArtScroll Siddur* comments, "The holy Presence of God rests with its greatest intensity between the Cherubim in the Holy of Holies in the Temple" (p. 313). Alternatively, S.D. Luzzatto takes a rationlist approach: "the ark's holiness was due to the tablets within it, not the cover and the cherubim" (on Exod. 25:21).

Spatial holiness is hierarchical but not concentric, since a person approaching from an opposite direction would bypass nearly all of these levels and immediately arrive at the Holy of Holies. Nonetheless, rabbinic homilies describe a concentric conception of the world, "The world is like a human eyeball. The white of the eye is the ocean surrounding the world, the iris is this continent, the pupil is Jerusalem, and the image in the pupil is the Holy Temple."[58]

After the destruction of the Temple, there are conflicting opinions of what happened to its holiness. R. Samuel b. Nahman says when the Temple was destroyed, the Divine Presence departed, while Rabbi Eleazar says the Divine Presence never left (*Exodus Rabbah* 2:2, quoted earlier). The debate between these two sages is intriguing from a theoretical perspective, but practically, after the Exile, the people could not find day-to-day solace in the belief that the Divine Presence never departed from the ruins of the Temple. The Rabbis focused on a verse from Ezekiel, "Therefore say, thus speaks the Lord God, when I distance them among the nations and when I scatter them in [foreign] lands, I shall be [*va-ehi*] for them a miniature sanctuary [*mikdash me'at*] in the lands they enter" (Ezek. 11:16). The Talmud adds: "Rabbi Isaac said these are the synagogues and study halls in Babylon. And Rabbi Elazar said this refers to the house of our Rabbi in Babylon.... Rabbi Elazar ha-Kappar says in the future the synagogues and study halls in Babylon will be reestablished in the land of Israel" (*Megillah* 29a). After the destruction of the Temple, the holiness of the Temple was, theologically, scattered to all the sanctuaries throughout the world. Rabbi Michael Taubes, by analogy, suggests that each synagogue is like an embassy

58. *Derekh Eretz Zuta* 9, quoted in Kaplan 1976: 5.

or consulate of the original sanctity of the Jerusalem Temple; just as an embassy is considered to be part of the country it represents, the sanctity of each synagogue is like the sanctity of the Temple.

Rabbi J. David Bleich draws another connection between the Temple and synagogue, and he quotes that the talmudic commentary *Mordekhai* "equated the sanctity of the synagogue with that of the Temple and asserts that both are biblical in nature" (1977: 62). Not just philosophically, but legally as well, the holiness of the Temple became extended to the holiness of the synagogue.

The sanctity of the altar is also extended: "While the Temple stood, the altar would atone [k-p-r] for man, but now that the Temple is not standing, a man's table atones for him" (*Hagigah* 27a, *Menahot* 97a). Rashi writes that the person's table atones for him when he feeds his guests (there is an implication of "poor guests"). In effect, Rashi is equating sacrifices to God with feeding the poor. Marcel Mauss, in his study of the Trobriand Islands, writes something similar, "The gods and spirits accept that the share of wealth and happiness that had been offered to them [the poor] and had been hitherto destroyed in useless sacrifices should serve the poor and children" (2000: 18). Charity, as a form of selflessness, can achieve atonement (see Dan. 4:24).[59] In a world where the possibility of ritual sacrifice is unavailable, the idea of atonement—and the altar itself—became a substitute for the Temple offerings.

---

59. Reading *tzidkah* as "charity" since it is a late biblical text.

Holiness of Times — Three Cycles

The Torah has three metrics of time: the weekly cycle, the yearly cycle, and the Jubilee cycle, and each shorter cycle is coiled within a longer one.

Weekly Cycle

Of the weekly cycle, every seventh day stands apart from the other six. The beginning of the Sabbath's sanctity is in the narrative of Creation, "And God blessed the seventh day and sanctified it" (Gen. 2:3). The Hebrew root *sh-b-t*, from which "Sabbath" is derived, means "cease, desist, rest." This root has lexical cognates in many other Semitic languages. Akkadian *šapattu* (or *šabattu*), means "fifteenth day of the month" (*CAD* Š), which is the festival of the full moon. Other cognates mean, variously, "cease, be completed," and "neglect." Although there is some debate about the lexical relationship between Akkadian šapattu and Hebrew *sh-b-t*, contextual evidence makes it clear that *šapattu* is not the origin for the biblical Sabbath. The biblical Israelite idea of Sabbath as cessation is unique.

Yearly Cycle

The second cycle is the yearly cycle of holiness, which has four levels of holiness: the intermediate days, the festival days, the Sabbath, and Yom Kippur. The intermediate festival days are holier than the ordinary days, and each set of intermediate days has restrictions. On the intermediate days of Passover, leaven is prohibited, and on the intermediate says of Sukkot, one may not eat outside the tabernacle. Certain labors are forbidden on these intermediate days as well. Maimonides writes, "The intermediate festival days, even though it is not said of them 'cessation [*shabbaton*],' since it has been called 'a proclamation of holiness,' it is thus a time of festivity in the Temple. The performance of creative work is prohibited, in order that [these days] not be like ordinary days that have no holiness whatsoever (*Hil. Yom Tov* 7:1). According to R. Vidal of Tolosa, author of the *Maggid Mishneh*, Maimonides believed all work was biblically permitted on these intermediate days, but the Sages prohibited work on these days so that they "not be like ordinary days" (see, however, *Lehem Mishneh*). Nahmanides espoused the more commonly held position that these prohibitions are biblical.[60]

The second rank contains the three Pilgrimage festivals and the New Year. Thirty-seven of the thirty-nine actions prohibited on the Sabbath apply also these Festivals. The penalty for violating a festival-day is lashes, which is lower than the penalty for Sabbath violation—death by either stoning or spiritual excision. These days are called *mikra'ei kodesh*, "convocations of holiness," which Onkelos translates as *me'arei kodesh*, "holy events." Nahmanides explains "that all people should come together on that day and be assembled to sanctify it, for it is a commandment upon Israel to be gathered together in God's House on the festival day to hallow it publicly with prayer and praise to God, and with clean garments, and to make it a day of feasting" (on Lev. 23:2). Seforno emphasizes that the holidays are a time when the Divine Presence reposes on Israel. S.D. Luzzatto says "*mikra kodesh* means a gathering

---

60. Nahmanides, *Hilkhot Hol ha-Mo'ed*. In the green, three-volume *Hiddushei ha-Ramban ha-Shalem*, it is printed after his comments on tractate *Megillah*.

and celebration of holiness, that is, for the honor of God" (on Exod. 12:16). Wright gives a possible meaning of "declaration of, call for, summoning to holiness" (1992: 243).

The third level is the Sabbath, on which all thirty-nine labors are forbidden, and the violator is punished with death by stoning (or spiritual excision), which means the Sabbath has an increased number of restrictions and a greater penalty for their violation. It is important to note the central place the Sabbath holds the Bible and rabbinic literature. Biblical lists of holidays begin by first mentioning the Sabbath, and the first time the root *k-d-sh* is ever used in the Bible is in reference to the Sabbath.

The fourth is the Day of Atonement. This day is called the Sabbath of Sabbaths, has additional prohibitions of eating, and a commandment of bodily affliction. However, even though Yom Kippur has more restrictions, the penalty for violating the Sabbath-like prohibitions is less severe than it is for a regular Sabbath (*Megillah* 7b). Thus the annual cycle has four levels of holiness—although perhaps only three are biblical—the intermediate festival days, the festival days, the Sabbath, and Yom Kippur.[61]

Jubilee Cycle

Holiness of seasons is also measured by the metric of the Jubilee cycle. The sabbatical year is called a Sabbath (Lev. 25:2), but is not called "holy." The Torah commands the Israelites to declare the Jubilee year "holy" (Lev. 25:10). Milgrom writes the Jubilee year "is sanctified by the positive act of proclamation by the blowing of a shofar—a rite of sanctification" (2000: 1399).

---

61. It is also possible that the New Moon once exhibited holiness that is not observed today.

Relationship of Time and Space

We have already seen that both places and times are subject to holiness. It is therefore necessary explore the relationship between the two. Peter Van Inwagen writes:

> Space and time are among the most puzzling of our concepts. And these two puzzling concepts seem to be inextricably linked. They are very different and yet there is sufficient similarity between them that, long before physicists decided that space and time were aspects of a single "space-time continuum," they were known intuitively to be two members, the only two members, of a kind of species (2009: 71).

He further notes that time and space share three properties, one of which is that they both have "continuity," which means they are both "intimately connected continua, intimately connected aspects of the physical world" (71). It will be instructive to see how holiness behaves in these two continua, keeping an eye for this shared property of continuity.

Regarding the relationship between time and space in the ancient Near East, Sarna writes:

> The polar contrast between Israelite and pagan concepts is vividly illustrated by the fact that the Mesopotamian "creation epic" known as *Enuma Elish* closes with the building of a temple to the god Marduk, that is, with the sanctification of space. In the Scriptural creation story, it is the sanctity of time—the Sabbath—that is first celebrated (1986: 41).

To be absolutely clear, Sarna is showing how the biblical narrative is a refutation of the surrounding culture. To this purpose, he concludes, "Only sacred time, not sacred space, partakes of the cosmic order" (214). The creation narratives—which describe how a civilization came to be—reverberate through that society and define its values. The thrust of Sarna's quotation is that holiness of time, represented biblically, is more profound than the pagan attribution of holiness to space. The primacy of time over space is reflected in the Jewish law as well. Rashi writes that maintenance of the Temple does not override the Sabbath (on Lev. 19:30), which demonstrates that holiness of time supersedes holiness of space.

The first time the root k-d-sh appears in the Bible is, "and God blessed the seventh day and hallowed it" (Gen. 2:3). There is a dearth of sources for sanctification in time in surrounding cultures,[62] while there are numerous sources for the sanctification of places, mostly temples and altars. It is obvious that in the ancient Near East, festivals were observed, but I have not found evidence that the root k-d-sh was applied to such occasions.[63]

---

62. Texts from Emar (east of modern-day Aleppo, Syria) refer to a "sanctification day" (Pentiuc 2001: 142), but this is more a day on which the sanctification of other objects occurs, rather than a day that is designated as holy. Surviving texts are obviously sparse, making any *argumentum ex silentio* treacherous.

63. For example, Del Olmo Lete writes about "sacred times," yet the texts he cites do not actually use the root k-d-sh in reference to those convocations. Ugaritic ritual texts frequently use the phrase *ytrḥs mlk brr*, "the king shall wash himself, becoming pure" (Del Olmo Lete 1999: 24), and this rite seems time-specific; additionally upon completing his rite, it says *wḥl mlk*, "and the king is desacralized" (see, e.g., Del Olmo Lete 1999: 107-111, Pardee 2002: 57, 106

The Bible also connects the ideas of time and place, "You shall keep My Sabbaths and revere My sanctuary; I am the Lord" (Lev. 19:30; 26:2). Seforno identifies the relationship of time and place in this verse, "He commanded us to honor the days and the places and the holy people" (on Lev. 19:30). Gammie writes that the Sabbath is "a sanctuary in time," and Joshua Berman calls it a "temporal shrine" (1977: 11), two locutions that blend the spatial with the temporal. Rabbi Moshe Shamah has also observed that when Moses blessed the tabernacle vessels (Exod. 39:43) and sanctified them (Exod. 40:9-13), it recalls that God blessed and sanctified the Sabbath (p. 503), which once again demonstrates how the holiness of time could be applied to the holiness of space.

According to Rabbi Shamah's reading, both continua—time and space—are sanctified: time in the creation narrative, and space in the construction of the tabernacle. The connection is consciously presented. Gammie also quotes from Childs, "The first account of the tabernacle closes with the Sabbath

---

n. 74). Del Olmo Lete writes about the king, "Before officiating as (sacrificial or oracular) 'priest,' the king 'washes himself, becoming purified.' ... Once this has taken places, corresponding to the ritual and temporal 'unit' (a day) in question, 'the sun sets and the king becomes desacralized [whl mlk]'... by why he 'returns' to the 'profane' state and time" (Del Olmo Lete 1999:37-38). Pardee further observes, "the use of ḤL(L) to designate the king's departure from his cultic responsibilities indicates that whatever 'sacredness' was attributed to kingship in general was not identical to cultic sacredness" (Pardee 2002: 237). The Hebrew Bible keeps the monarchy and priesthood as discrete offices, as Uzziah (King Azariah) was punished for usurping the sacerdotal role by burning incense (2 Chron. 26:18). Perhaps this is because only God can combine holiness and kingship (see Isa. 43:15).

command [and] the second account of its building begins with the Sabbath command" (1991: 20). Gorman notes, "Just as rituals cannot be performed at just any place, so they cannot be performed at just any time" (1990: 57-58). The Rabbis also connected them in a legal context, deriving the Sabbath prohibitions from the acts required to construct and maintain the Tabernacle (*Shabbat* 49b). The connection between time and space is strengthened on both exegetical and legal grounds.

Ezekiel uses language to show that both space and time are subject to desecration, "Furthermore this they have done to me: they have defiled [*t-m-'*] My sanctuary on that day, and My Sabbaths they have profaned [*ḥ-l-l*]" (Ezek. 23:38, which likely referenced Lev. 19:30, 26:2). The sanctity of time and place has both a positive fulfillment and a negative violation. The root *ḳ-d-sh* can describe the positive fulfillment of both time and place, but time and place have some terms that are unique. Desecration of holy times is represented by *ḥ-l-l*, but defilement of holy places is represented by *t-m-'*.

The relationship between holiness of time and place is also present in a mystical notion that the Sabbath is not the last day of the week; rather it is the middle day (fourth day) of the week, which three days preceding it and three days following it. R. Bahya takes this position in his comments on Exod. 12:2-3. It is a mystical notion, but it represents the idea that time and space are related. Just as space has gradations, it is suggested that time also has gradients. This can be extended, with some speculation, to say that according to this notion, the first three and last three days of the week may serve as a progressive entrance and incremental departure of temporal holiness to and from the Sabbath day. This interpretation, it seems, is loosely based on the connection between space and time that must have existed even in ancient and medieval times. It certainly is a unique and compelling application of Van Inwagen's thesis that time and space are "inextricably linked."

Holiness of Offerings

The levels of animal sacrifices are by law two, *kodshei kodashim* (most holy offerings) and *kodashim kalim* (lesser holy offerings). The *kodshei kodashim* are the *asham*, *hatta't*, and *olah*, all of which have an expiatory function.[64] The sacrifices of greater holiness divide into two types, and the nomenclature does not confer this extremely important difference. The *olah* is immolated on the altar, and the *Midrash Tanḥuma* believes "the *olah* is superior [*elyonah*] to all sacrifices because no creature partakes of it" (cf. Milgrom 1991: 174). The *asham* and *hatta't* are consumed by the priests. These offerings have additional restrictions in that they can only be eaten within the Temple precincts and only on the day the animals are slaughtered. It is worth emphasizing that the most holy offerings have an atoning function, while the lesser offerings serve other purposes. Furthermore, the priests, in consuming the *asham* and *hatta't*, appear to stand in the place of God.

The lower offerings, including *shelamim*, *bekhorot*, *ma'aser*, and *Pesaḥ* (loosely: peace-offering, firstborn, tithe, and Paschal offerings), are permitted to ritually pure Israelites, but must be consumed within the walls of Jerusalem, which is a spatial restriction.

---

64. The names of these sacrifices are almost untranslatable, but *asham* has been translated "guilt offering," *hatta't* as "sin offering" or "purgation offering," and *olah* as "elevation offering."

The Torah restricts the animals that the layman may eat to ten species (Deut. 14:4-5). There is no species that is prohibited to the laity that can be offered as a sacrifice. Only three permitted species of mammals may be brought on the altar, despite a much greater variety allowed to the laymen. Likewise, only two types or birds are brought in the Temple, and no fishes, despite the larger numbers allowed to the commoners. This observation affirms that the holy is more restrictive than the ordinary (see Josh. 6:24-26). Mary Douglas gives a useful example, although it is quite confused: "What may be burned on the altar may be burned in the kitchen; what may be consumed by the altar may be consumed by the body. The dietary laws intricately model the body and the altar upon one another" (2002: xv-xvi). The Temple may correspond to the human body, but the two are distinguishable. For the most part, the Temple has more restrictions that the laity, with two exceptions: *melikah* and *ḥēlev*.

Melikah (Lev. 1:15) is a process where the priest inserts his fingernail in the back of a bird's neck in order to slaughter it as part of a sacrifice. This, however, may be little more than an act to reduce the likelihood of the sacrifice becoming invalid, since avian sacrifices can be easily mishandled. Second, the forbidden fats (*ḥēlev*) of species fit for the altar are regarded as prohibited, and cannot be eaten, but are burned on the altar. Hence, Douglas is wrong in writing, "what may be consumed by the altar may be consumed by the body," since the two examples of *melikah* and *ḥēlev* refute her thesis.

Correspondent Holiness

Analysis of the blueprint of the Tabernacle reveals an elaborate system of correspondence between various levels of sanctity. This hierarchy extends to inanimate objects, in the materials that are used in the differing sections of the Tabernacle. This incorporates the metals used for Tabernacle accoutrements, the metals used for the sockets delimiting the boundaries, the fabrics used, the weaves and stitching used for the differing regions, and the types of garments that are worn.

The sockets of the Tabernacle correspond to the level of holiness. Sarna writes: "the wooden posts that marked the perimeter of the Court were inserted into bronze sockets, whereas those that delimited the inner rectangle rested in silver sockets. The clasps of the outer, or upper, curtains were made of bronze; those of the inner, or lower, curtains were of gold" (1986: 205).

This can also be measured in the types of fabrics used. As Gammie said, this means that holiness is "color coded" (1989: 16). Milgrom notes that the order is always *tekhelet*, "violet" (blue-purple); *argaman*, "purple" (or red-purple); and *tola'at shani*, "crimson" (1990: 25). This also probably corresponds to the acts of weaving and embroidery such as *ḥ-r-sh*, *ḥ-sh-b*, and *r-ḳ-m* (see Exod. 38:23)

Another graded holiness appears in the garments that are worn. Milgrom opines that the prohibition of *sha'atnez*, the mixture of wool and linen, applies differently to the High Priest, the priests, and the Israelites. The High Priest wears an outer garment of *sha'atnez*, while the priests are only permitted a sash made from *sha'atnez*. The Israelites are permitted *sha'atnez* on their *tzitzit*, a dispensation that Milgrom explains is "a reminder that he should aspire to a life of holiness" (1991: 549). *Sha'atnez* seems to be a privilege of holiness. It may not be worn by the commoner, save in the *tzitzit*; but the priests must wear garments made of this mixture.[65]

All of these rules can be mapped out in the following chart:

	Gradations of Holiness		
Place	Outer Court	Holy Place	Holy of Holies
People	Israelites	Priests	High Priest
Time	Bringing sacrificial animal to the Tabernacle/ Temple	Officiating	Officiating during Yom Kippur
Offerings	Lesser Holy Offerings	Greater Holy Offerings	Incense
Metals	Copper	Lined in Pure Gold	Solid Pure Gold
Sockets	Wood and Bronze	Silver	Gold
Color	*Tola'at shani*	*Argaman*	*Tekhelet*
Type of Weave	*r-ḳ-m*	*ḥ-sh-b*	*ḥ-r-sh*

Liminal Items

We have seen that there are five metrics of holiness: times, places, people, animals, and inanimate objects. The holiness of times, places, and people have a liminality, a threshold

---

65. Milgrom's thesis is the inverse of that taken by Maimonides, who says that wool and linen was a common idolatrous mixture, so the Torah forbade it to eradicate idolatry (see *Guide* 3:37).

between differing ranks. This liminality is intuitive, since these thresholds are often the protective borders for what enters these holy times, places, and people. Douglas has argued convincingly that holiness is often defined as that which traverses the body, especially the buccal and genital orifices. Her insight is accurate, but it needs to be fleshed out.

Liminality of the Priests

When Aaron and his sons were consecrated, they were not permitted to leave the door of the tent of meeting for a week, "And at the door of the tent of meeting you shall abide day and night seven days, and keep the charge of the Lord, that you not die..." (Lev. 8:35). This restriction to the common is for a specific purpose. The priests were in a liminal state, in the process of entering the nascent priesthood. They had to dwell in the doorway, the very symbol of transition. Once Aaron and his sons had their priestly status in place, they were again permitted to move about the entire camp like any Israelite.[66]

Wright, quoting from anthropologists van Gennep and Leach, explains, "many rituals that involve movement in social status often have a threefold division: (1) rites of separation where the subject is demarcated from his or her surroundings by actual removal or symbolic rites (disrobing-clothing, purification, etc.), (2) a marginal or liminal period—of 'social timelessness'—of long or short duration which often continues the subject's separation with prohibitions to be observed and which may be accompanied by rites, and (3) rites of aggregation or incorporation where persons return to their previous state or, at least, having a new social status, to a state of integration with society" (1992: 247).

---

66. See Milgrom 1991: 504, 538. For further references on liminality in general, see Milgrom 2001: 1951-2.

Liminality of the Sabbath

The Sabbath also has a liminality about it, certainly by the time of Rabbinic Judaism. These are the *kiddush*, which is recited at or near the entrance of the Sabbath, and *havdalah*, recited at or after the Sabbath's departure.[67] Thus the transitions to the Sabbath and from it are actively, not passively, experienced. The *kiddush* and *havdalah* introduce the liminality of time (see Maimonides, *ShM*, Pos. 155).

More broadly, Rabbi Gil Student quotes from Rabbi Jacob Ettlinger: "*Havdalah*, distinguishing between sacred and profane, between right and wrong, between good and evil, forms one of our primary challenges in life. The inability to differentiate between legitimate and illegitimate Torah interpretations is a sign of a crippled critical mind. It is a paralysis of judgment that quickly and inevitably leads to religious collapse" (2018: 310).

Liminality of the Body

As for the liminality of the body itself, such items can be a source of impurity or holiness. Food and drink are liminal items, since they traverse the body through the mouth: "You shall not make yourselves abominable with any creeping abomination, and you shall not defile yourselves and be defiled by them. For I am the Lord your God, and you shall sanctify yourselves and shall be holy, because I am holy, and you shall not defile yourselves with any abomination that swarms on the ground" (Lev. 11:43-44).

---

67. See also *Pesaḥim* 102b, which says that "*kiddush* and *havdalah* are considered one matter," although that is in a case where the *havdalah* is being recited in a transition from the Sabbath to a festival day on the subsequent day.

The same is true of the intimate organs of the body. A woman's menses and a man's emission are sources of impurity, and Leviticus 18 lists the forbidden sexual relations, and according to one rabbinic tradition, quoted by Rashi, the call to holiness in Lev. 19:2 is a summation of the list of forbidden relations.

Hair is also a liminal item, for example concerning the Levites, the priests, and the Nazirites. The hair of the Levites is fully removed, while the hair of the priests and the Nazirites is treated as holy. In the latter two cases, the hair seems to be a synecdoche for the head, and by extension the symbol of life itself. Milgrom quotes that Persia and India regarded cut hair and nails as impure; the latter also likened human feces as impure. Maimonides further writes that: "Another custom among the Sabeans, which is still widespread, is this: whatever is separated from the body, as hair, nail, or blood, is unclean; every barber is therefore unclean in their estimation, because he touches blood and hair; whenever a person passes a razor over his skin he must take a bath in running water" (*Guide* 3:47).

Another liminal item is spittle. The crucial verse discussing it is, "And if a *zav* spits upon one that is clean, then he shall wash his clothes and bathe himself in water, and he shall be clean until evening" (Lev. 15:8). The question seems to be what drives the verse: the spittle or the state of being a *zav*? The Mishnah is clear that only spittle of the *zav* is unclean, to the exception of other expectorates (*Niddah* 7:1; Maimonides, *Mishkav u-Moshav* 2:1), but not spittle in general.

The Bible makes no mention of the impurity of fingernails nor onychomancy. However, the Talmud has a curious statement: "Three things were said in reference to nails: One who buries them is righteous; one who burns them is pious and one who throws them away is a villain. What is the reason? Lest a pregnant woman should step over them and miscarry" (*Mo'ed Katan* 18a), which mystically is connected with the idea of *kelippot* (husks of impurity). The *Mishnah Berurah* does not quote the idea of *kelippot*, but reiterates that a person who has cut his nails should perform a ritual hand-washing, akin to the washing upon waking, before eating bread, and before prayer (260:7).

Speech Acts

What does it mean to sanctify something? Here the idea of "speech-acts" becomes relevant. A speech-act is an utterance that effects a certain result. John Austin popularized the concept of speech-acts in his work, and though his terminology is needlessly complex and often unclear, one can categorize utterances into two types: "descriptive" utterances and "performative" utterances.[68] Descriptive utterances describe a pre-existing state, though sometimes they remind or inspire the addressee. Performative utterances bring about a new state or condition. This tension was already noted by the talmudic discussion whether speech is considered an act or not (*amirah ke-ma'aseh dami*).[69] In applying Austin's methods, a clearer distinction can be attained; sometimes an utterance describes a state, and sometimes an utterance or declaration creates a state.

Kornfeld identifies three meanings of *k-d-sh* in *pi'el*. The first is, "bring something/someone into the condition of holiness/consecration according to the cultic regulation." The

---

68. I am using "descriptive" and "performative" in lieu of "illocutionary" and "perlocutionary."

69. Compare *amirato le-Gavohah ki-mesirato le-hedyiot* (*Kiddushin* 1:6, *Avodah Zarah* 63a) and *kedushat peh* (*Pesahim* 34b), and Maimonides' statement that "sticks, stones, dirt, and dust become holy as soon as the name of the Master of the Universe is called upon them with words alone" (*Me'ilah* 8:8)

second is "declaring something/someone holy." The third is "considering/viewing something/someone as holy" (p. 528).

Kornfeld's three categories of k-d-sh in the pi'el harmonize well with these two categories of speech-acts. Kornfeld's first category, "bring something/someone into the condition of holiness/consecration," is not a speech-act at all, but a physical act, such as anointing, washing, or donning certain garments; these acts can be executed without any recitation. The second category, "declaring something/someone holy," is a performative speech-act, since it verbally generates a new state of holiness. The third category, "considering/viewing something/someone as holy," is a descriptive utterance, since it informs or reminds the addressee of a pre-existing state or condition of holiness. This analysis can be represented in the following chart:

Kornfeld: Use of *Pi'el*	**Austin: Type of Speech-Act**
"bring someone/something into the condition of holiness/consecration according to cultic regulation"	Not applicable. This is a physical act, not a speech-act
"declaring something/ someone holy"	Performative utterance—creates a new state
"considering/viewing something/someone as holy"	Descriptive utterance— describes a pre-existing state (achieved either by a physical act or a speech-act), for either informational or emotive purposes.

Based on this scheme, some redundancies can be explained, and some ambiguities can be clarified.

127

Speech Acts and the Sabbath

When God sanctified the Sabbath (Gen. 2:3), He imbued it with holiness, which is a performative utterance, which is not the case when the Israelites sanctify the Sabbath (e.g., Exod. 20:8). According to some opinions, sanctification is achieved by ceasing from menial, servile, or constructive labor; the sanctification is an action (the *in*action, the act of cessation), not an utterance. The *Tanḥuma* explains, "The house of Israel is obligated to rest on the Sabbath day, and the Merciful One said to us, 'You shall rest on the Sabbath day just as I rested on it.' As it is written, 'Remember the seventh day to sanctify it.'" Accordingly, the Sabbath is sanctified by the act of rest; sanctification requires that action.

Alternatively Maimonides writes, "It is a biblical commandment to sanctify the Sabbath with words" (*Hil. Shabbat* 29:1). According to this opinion, to sanctify the Sabbath is a speech-act. This explains the rhetorical dictum of the Talmud: "Does Israel sanctify the Sabbath? But the Sabbath was already sanctified [at Creation]" (*Betzah* 17a). God *made* the Sabbath holy, but the Jews announce the pre-existing holiness.

Similarly, regarding the Jubilee, Ibn Ezra and Maimonides (*ShM*, Pos. 136) understand this as a reference to cessation of labor. However, Rashi understands that the sanctification is a public declaration; for him, declaring the Jubilee holy is a performative utterance.

Speech Acts and the Priests

Concerning the priests, God, Moses, and the Israelites all sanctify the priests in their own way. Moses sanctifies the priests, "And you shall put [the clothing] upon Aaron thy brother, and upon his sons with him... and sanctify them" (Exod. 28:41). This physical act of enrobing and anointing may be what embues them with holiness[70] (Kornfeld's first category). God sanctifies the priests, "I will sanctify Aaron and his sons to minister to Me" (Exod. 29:44), which is a performative utterance (second category). The Israelites are also commanded to sanctify Aaron (Lev. 21:8), which means they must "treat" or "regard" him as holy (third category).

Speech Acts and Firstborn Animals

There is a purported contradiction concerning the sanctification of the firstborn. In one place it says, "All the firstborn males that are born of your herd and of your flock you shall sanctify unto the Lord your God" (Deut. 15:19, cf. Exod. 13:2). However, elsewhere it is stated, "Only the firstborn of the beasts… no man shall sanctify it" (Lev. 27:26). Rashi resolves the contradiction by saying that the owner cannot sanctify the animal for another purpose because God has already sanctified the animal as the status of "firstborn." Nahmanides, however, says there is no need to sanctify it because it is automatically sanctified; the implication is that there is no need to sanctify it verbally (second category). And in Deuteronomy, which states, "You shall sanctify unto the Lord your God," Nahmanides says that means "you are to treat it with holiness, so that you are not to do work with it, nor shear it and that you are to eat it before Lord" (on Lev. 27:26). Concerning Deut. 15:19, Chavel adds a footnote, "This verse does not mean that the owner is to declare it 'holy' [i.e., a performative utterance], since it is automatically holy by virtue of being the firstborn, but as Ramban continues, that we are to regard it has holy" (Lev. p. 477 n. 194). S.D.

---

70. Following Nahmanides (Lev. 16:32); however Ibn Ezra says the sanctification was verbal (Exod. 28:41).

Luzzatto take a position diametrically opposed to Nahmanides, and undersands the phrase *kaddesh li* as sanctify to Me by "oral statement" (on Exod. 8:22), which means that the sanctity of the firstborn is not generated or is at least unrealized until the verbal declaration is made.

What God Sanctifies & What Man Sanctifies
The Bible speaks of seven things that God sanctifies: the Sabbath, the priests, the Israelites, the Temple (or Tabernacle),[71] the prophet Jeremiah, the firstborns, and God's name. In six of these seven cases, there is a parallel verse that humans sanctified the same object, as summarized on the opposite page. (The top row shows when God sanctifies the object; the bottom row shows when man sanctifies it.)

Some of these parallels have been employed in the argument that the Bible endorses the idea of *imitatio Dei*, but based on our analysis of speech-acts, it should be clear that the root *k-d-sh* can have different meanings, per Kornfeld and Austin, which illuminates the fact that when God sanctifies something and when man sanctifies something (i.e., that same thing), the meaning of "sanctify" is not the same in both cases.

---

71. The terms *mishkan* and *mikdash* are interchangeable (*Eruvin* 2a-b).

Firstborn	His Name	Jeremiah	Temple/Place of Worship	Israelites	Priests	Sabbath
On the day that I smote all the first-born in the land of Egypt I sanctified them for Myself (Num. 8:17).	And I will sanctify My great name (Ezek. 36:23).	Before you came forth out of the womb I sanctified you (Jer. 1:5).	And I will sanctify the tent of meeting (Exod. 29:44; cf 2 Chron. 7:16).	My statutes, and do them: I am the Lord who sanctifies you (Lev. 20:8).	Aaron also and his sons will I sanctify. (Exod. 29:44)	And God blessed the seventh day, and hallowed it (Gen. 2:3).
All the firstborn males that are born of your herd and of your flock you shall sanctify unto the Lord your God (Deut. 15:19, see also Exod. 13:2).	They shall sanctify My name (Isa. 29:23).	(—)	Solomon hallowed the middle of the court that was before the house of the Lord (2 Chron. 7:7).	Sanctify yourselves, and be holy (Lev. 11:44).	And you shall put [the clothing] upon Aaron your brother, and upon his sons with him… and sanctify them (Exod. 28:41).	Observe the Sabbath day, to keep it holy (Deut 5:11).

Chapter 7

Biblical Understanding of "Being Holy"

In many places, the Bible either prophesies or commands about the Israelites being holy:

- "And you shall be for Me a kingdom of priests and a holy nation" (Exod. 19:6).
- "And you shall be a holy people to Me…" (Exod. 22:30)
- "You shall sanctify yourselves and you shall be holy… You shall be holy, for I am holy"
  (Lev. 11:44-45).
- "… You shall be holy, because I the Lord your God am holy" (Lev. 19:2).
- "Make yourselves holy and be holy, for I am the Lord your God" (Lev. 20:7).
- "And you shall be holy to Me; for I the Lord am holy, and I have set you apart from the nations to be Mine" (Lev. 20:26).
- "That you will remember and will do all My commandments and be holy to the Lord your God" (Num. 15:40).
- "You are a people holy to the Lord your God" (Deut. 7:6; the use of *am ḳadosh attah la-YHVH* appears numerous times in Deuteronomy).

- "You are a people holy to the Lord your God" (Deut. 14:1; this phrase is verbatim of Deut. 7:6, though the context is different).

- "You shall not eat anything that dies of itself; you may give it to aliens residing in your towns for them to eat, or you may sell it to a foreigner. For you are a people holy to the Lord your God. You shall not boil a kid in its mother's milk" (Deut. 14:21).

- "Today the Lord has obtained your agreement: to be His treasured people, as He promised you, and to keep His commandments; for Him to set you high above all nations that He has made, in praise and in fame and in honor; and for you to be a people holy to the Lord your God, as He promised" (Deut. 26:18-19).

- "The Lord will establish you as His holy people, as He has sworn to you, if you keep the commandments of the Lord your God and walk in His ways" (Deut. 28:9).

- "Indeed, O favorite among peoples, all His holy ones were in your charge; they marched at your heels, accepted direction from you. Moses charged us with the law, as a possession for the assembly of Jacob" (Deut 33:3-4; which might refer to angels, not people).

These verses are inherently pliable, but in each case, the passage explicitly endorses following the biblical laws, either in whole or in part. Before we analyze the opinion of later authorities, it is essential to read the texts on their own, and observe what concepts are linked to holiness, remaining focused on the legal consequence of each verse:

Citation	Verse	
Exod. 19:5-6	Now therefore, if you obey my voice and keep My covenant, you shall be My treasured possession out of all the peoples. Indeed, the whole earth is mine, but you shall be for Me a priestly kingdom and a holy nation. These are the words that you shall speak to the Israelites.	
Exod. 22:30	You shall be people consecrated to Me; therefore you shall not eat any meat that is mangled by beasts in the field; you shall throw it to the dogs.	
Lev. 11:44-45	For I am the Lord your God; sanctify yourselves therefore, and be holy, for I am holy. You shall not defile yourselves with any swarming creature that moves on the earth. For I am the Lord who brought you up from the land of Egypt, to be your God; you shall be holy, for I am holy.	
Lev. 19:2	Speak to all the congregation of the people of Israel and say to them: You shall be holy, for I the Lord your God am holy.	
Lev. 20:7	Consecrate yourselves therefore, and be holy; for I am the Lord your God.	
Lev. 20:26	You shall be holy to Me; for I the Lord am holy, and I have separated you from the other peoples to be Mine.	
Num. 15:40	So you shall remember and do all My commandments, and you shall be holy to your God.	
Deut. 7:6	For you are a people holy to the Lord your God; the Lord your God has chosen you out of all the peoples on earth to be His people, His treasured possession.	
Deut. 14:1-2	You are children of the Lord your God. You must not lacerate yourselves or shave your forelocks for the dead. For you are a people holy to the Lord your God; it is you the Lord has chosen out of all the peoples on earth to be His people, His treasured possession.	

Call to Holiness	Legal Consequence
be... a holy nation	if you obey My voice = follow entire Torah
You shall be a people consecrated to Me	you shall not eat any meat that is mangled
sanctify yourselves therefore, and be holy	Cannot eat swarming creatures
You shall be holy	Either sexual laws (Lev. 18) or the list of commandments at Lev. 19
Consecrate yourselves	v. 6 prohibits idolatry; v. 8 reiterates all commandments.[2]
You shall be holy to Me	v. 25 discusses prohibited food; v. 27 prohibits idolatry
you shall be holy	do all My commandments
you are a people holy to the Lord	v. 5 prohibits idolatry
you are a people holy to the Lord	v. 1 prohibits actions that were probably based on idolatrous rites (e.g., 1 Kings 18:28).

Deut. 26:17-19	Today you have obtained the Lord's agreement: to be your God; and for you to walk in His ways, to keep His statutes, His commandments, and His ordinances, and to obey Him. Today the Lord has obtained your agreement: to be His treasured people, as He promised you, and to keep His commandments; for Him to set you high above all nations that He has made, in praise and in fame and in honour; and for you to be a people holy to the Lord your God, as He spoke.	
Deut. 28:9	The Lord will establish you as His holy people, as He has sworn to you, if you keep the commandments of the Lord your God and walk in His ways.	
Deut. 33:3-4	Indeed, O favorite among peoples, all His holy ones were in your charge; they marched at your heels, accepted direction from you. Moses charged us with the law, as a possession for the assembly of Jacob.	

Based on this assessment, the following statistics can be collected:

- Holiness refers to keeping *all of the commandments* explicitly in four places (Exod. 19:5-6, Num. 15:40, Deut. 26:17-19, Deut. 28:9), and perhaps in another three verses (Lev. 19:2, Lev. 20:7,[72] Deut. 33:3-4).

- Holiness refers to *dietary laws* explicitly twice (Exod. 22:30, Lev. 11:44-45), and perhaps also Lev. 20:26.

- Holiness refers to the *prohibition of idolatry* twice (Deut. 7:5-6, Deut. 14:1-2), and perhaps also Lev. 20:7 and Lev. 20:26.

---

72. Commentaries are split on whether v. 7 concludes v. 6 or introduces v. 8.

for you to be a people holy to the Lord	v. 17 requires following the Torah
The Lord will establish you as His holy people	keep the commandments of the Lord
Favorite among His peoples, His holy ones	Moses charged us with the law

Every time the Israelites are commanded or prophesied to be holy, it is directly tied to keeping the entire Torah, observing the dietary laws, or abstaining from idolatry. Other theories of holiness, which developed later, may have roots or corollaries from the Bible, but they are not the central biblical theme of the Israelites' holiness.

Holiness & Sexuality

R. Judah b. Pazzi, a fourth-century (CE) Palestinian rabbi, taught, "wherever one finds the limitations of sexuality, one finds [mention of] holiness" (*Leviticus Rabbah* 24:6). This dictum is well known because Rashi quotes it on "you shall be holy" (Lev. 19:2). The question is when sexuality came to be called by the term "holy," since as shown in the previous section, the two concepts are never explicitly linked.

Even though proper sexual conduct is never *explicitly* linked with holiness, sexual conduct has the effect of causing defilement. The Bible declares, "if a man has an emission of semen, he shall wash himself with water, and be unclean until the evening" (Lev. 15:16); the woman he had relations with is also impure on a biblical level until the evening (Lev. 15:18), and rabbincally for three days (M. *Miḳva'ot* 8:3). Additionally, both a menstruant and woman who has given birth (a parturient) are impure. There is ample evidence that seminal emissions, menstruation, and childbirth are defiling, not just in the Bible, but in the ancient Near East and worldwide as well (see e.g., Milgrom 1991: 763-768).[73]

Improper sexual conduct is called impure, and it seems there is an exhortative component to this statement in addition to a ritual component. It is true that, from a strict legal perspective, sex defiles due to certain biological functions, but in other places, the context is clearly not legal, but more general, "Do not defile yourselves by any of these [sexual unions] because by all of these the nations were defiled which I cast out from before you. And the land will be defiled, and I will visit its iniquity on it, and the land itself will spit out its inhabitants" (Lev. 18:24-25).[74] None of these sources explicitly connect sexuality with

73. Regarding the ancient Near East, Van der Toorn suggests, "normal sexual intercourse brough about impurity and necessitated ritual ablutions" (1985:32), and he gives the example where the gods "Nergal and Ereškigal engage in ritual ablutions after their love-making" (1985: 170-171 n. 288).
74. This is Nahmanides' source for holiness as proper sexual conduct.

holiness, only with impurity. Since these intimate activities can be defiling, it follows that they require purification. But purity is not yet holiness, so the question remains when sexual conduct was defined in terms of holiness.

Two biblical sources may serve to connect the idea of holiness and sexuality for non-priests. One is the preparation for Sinai, where it says, "And the Lord said to Moses, 'Go to the people and sanctify them today and tomorrow'.... And Moses went down the mountain to the people and sanctified the people.... And he said to the people, 'Be prepared for the third day and *do not approach a woman*'" (Exod. 19:10-15). Maimonides, for example, sees this as the source that sanctification consists in the absence of sensuality (*Guide* 3:33).[75]

Another possible source is, "For the Lord your God walks in the midst of your camp, to save you and to give up your enemies before you; therefore your camp shall be holy; that He see *no unseemly thing* [*ervat davar*] in you and turn away from you" (Deut. 23:15).[76] Nahmanides, quoting a Midrash, writes,

75. Many people, including Maimonides, in his description of the Nazir, says that separation from wine is called holiness (Num. 6:4, *Guide* 3:33; also Kimhi on Ps. 34:10). Putting it all together, it has also been pointed out that wine increases the desire for sexual activity (*Minḥat Shai* on 1 Sam. 1:9).

76. There are four places where the mention of holiness is mentioned in proximity to sexual activity, yet these do not seem definitive. First is the list of forbidden sexual practices (Leviticus 18), followed by the commandment to be holy (Lev. 19:2). However, since Leviticus 19:1 clearly demarcates the beginning of a new unit, that juxtaposition is compromised. Second is that Leviticus 19 includes the prohibition, "You shall not prostitute your daughter, to turn her into a whore" (Lev. 19:29). Third is Leviticus 11, which concludes with "sanctify yourselves and be holy" (Lev. 11:44), while the next chapter (Leviticus 12) discusses

"It says *ervah* [an unseemly thing] — just as *ervah* uniquely represents a deed for which the Canaanites were driven from the Land and which removes the Divine Presence [from Israel], so all deeds for which the Canaanites were driven from the Land and which remove the Divine Presence [from Israel] are included in the admonition of this verse" (on Deut. 23:10).

Both of these passages describe a specific event. Exodus 19 discusses the theophany at Sinai, and Deut. 23:15 is guidance for how to be successful in battle; proper sexual conduct in these cases is called holiness.[77] However, there is no biblical verse that explicitly calls sexuality "holy" which is not case-specific. While this sentiment did not develop until a later stage in history, one can easily see how this is rooted in the Bible.

Rabbi Soloveitchik also quotes from the *Iggeret ha-Kodesh*, "Intercourse is holy and pure when it takes place in the proper manner, at the proper time, and with the proper attitude. And no one should say that there is anything bad or ugly about

the parturient. Fourth is Leviticus 20, which collectively prohibits forbidden sexual activities, forbidden foods, and séances (i.e., forbidden worship), and also mentions holiness (vv. 7, 26). Despite this proximity, sexual activity is not explicitly called holy in this chapter.

77. It is misleading to say that these cases are "called holiness." In Exodus 19, holiness is not explicitly mentioned (though strongly implied) as the reason men should separate from their wives. In Deut. 23:15, Milgrom understands holiness as a reference to "residual impurity to wear off totally—the day must end before the soldier can regain admittance" (Milgrom 1990: 385); in other words, "holy" in this verse means simply "free from impurity." Rashi, in his commentary on the Talmud, does not even connect holiness to sexual behavior; rather he says the camp is holy because the Israelites were always learning Torah (*Shabbat* 150a, s.v. *ve-hayah maḥanekha ḳadosh*).

intercourse, Heaven forbid, since it is called 'knowledge' [in the Scriptures], as it is said, 'And Elkanah knew his wife Hannah' (1 Sam. 1:19)" (2008: 198).

Holiness & Food

Forbidden foods are explicitly linked with the notion of holiness (Exod. 22:30, Lev. 11:44-45, and perhaps also Lev. 20:26). Other ancient Near Eastern cultures had foods it regarded as undesirable. In Akkadian, the pig (*šaḫu*) is called *la qašid*, which has been translated as both "unclean" (*CAD*) and "unholy" (*BWL*). Though porcine sacrifice was forbidden, and the animal was considered an abomination, it was not technically forbidden to consume. Van der Toorn suggests, "These 'unclean' animals were not under all circumstances prohibited as food. Although pigs provoked a general disgust, pork was a dish commonly enjoyed" (1985: 34-35).

The *Letter of Aristeas*, which dates to the second century BCE, explains:

> … all the rules which he has laid down with regard to what is permitted in the case of these birds and other animals, he has enacted with the object of teaching us a moral lesson. For the division of the hoof and the separation of the claws are intended to teach us that we must discriminate between our individual actions with a view to the practice of virtue…. [Also] we have been distinctly separated from the rest of mankind. For most other men defile themselves by promiscuous intercourse, thereby working great iniquity, and whole

countries and cities pride themselves upon such vices. For they not only have intercourse with men but they defile their own mothers and even their daughters. But we have been kept separate from such sins (149-153).

Here holiness is not only linked to the dietary laws, but to proper sexual conduct as well.

Holiness & Idolatry

The prohibition of idolatry is also called by the term holiness, "And the soul which turns to mediums and wizards to lust [z-n-h] after them, I will set My face against that soul and I will cut him off from among his people. Sanctify yourselves and be holy because I am the Lord your God" (Lev. 20:6-7; also Lev. 20:26-27; possibly Lev. 19:4 and v. 31).

Rashi's comment on this verse can be regarded as the simple meaning of the verse, "Sanctify yourselves: this is separation [perishut] from idolatry." Rabbi Samson Raphael Hirsch notes that there is a "special [form of] holiness which is to be sought and kept by keeping away from all forms of idolatrous practices" (on Lev. 20:7).

Relationship Between Sex, Food, and Idolatry

One can make a conceptual argument that the two strongest urges a person has are for food and sex. Maimonides makes this argument, writing, "in these two matters, God has separated us from the other nations" (Introduction to *Mishneh Torah*; also *Aristeas* 151-152, quoted above). Furthermore, food supports the individual, while sex sustains the species, so one would expect those to be mankind's most basic impulses.

Historically, Jewish tradition teaches that the desire for idolatry was stronger than either of these, and one could profitably argue that the spiritual survival is even more important than the physical perpetuation of the species. Perhaps for this reason, the word *zenut* is used for both forbidden sexual activity and idolatry (e.g., Lev. 19:29 and 20:5). According to Seforno, the concern may be that intermarriage *will lead to idolatry* (Deut. 7:6). Harvey makes a similar argument: "Ceremonies involving sex and food were fundamental to ancient Canaanite idolatry no less than to modern idolatry. Separating ourselves from forbidden sex and forbidden foods, we in effect separate ourselves from idolatrous practices involving sex and food" (1977: 16).

From a biblical perspective, man can sanctify himself by observing the dietary laws, and by being attentive to the laws of idolatry, while the idea of sanctification through proper sexual conduct is implied from either Exod. 19:10-15 (Maimonides), Leviticus 18-19 (Rashi, Nahmanides), or Deut. 23:15. We have shown above that many verses demanding holiness refer to observance of all the commandments. These verses indicate that these three commandments—proper sexual conduct, observance of dietary laws, and eschewing all forms of false worship—are singled out under the banner of holiness.

Holiness and Justice

Some have argued that *k-d-sh* is an amoral term.[78] Others have the view that *k-d-sh* is characterized as a capricious, demonic,

---

78. Snaith quotes from Nöldeke in Snaith 1964: 31; see also Lasine 2010:42-48, and Otto 5-7.

and destructive force that might kill or wound indiscriminately. A third view is that it as a primarily moral term.[79]

The third-millennium Sumerian "Hymn to Enlil, the All-Beneficent" opens with the words, "Enlil whose command is far-reaching, lofty is his word and holy," and the entire poem describes the city's admirable qualities. Among its merits is that "Hypocrisy, distortion, abuse, malice, unseemliness, insolence, enmity, oppression, envy, brute force, libelous speech, arrogance, violation of agreement, breach of contract, abuse of a court verdict are not tolerated by the city" (cf. *ANET* 573, ll. 20-26). This hymn repeatedly emphasizes the moral imperative that the city of Nippur requires, presumably stemming from Enlil's holiness.

In the Pentateuch and early prophets there are some hints to holiness and righteousness, but that does not seem to be developed until later. In fact, in the Hebrew Bible the roots *ḳ-d-sh* and *tz-d-ḳ* (as in *tzedakah*, i.e., "righteousness") do appear together occasionally (e.g., Isa. 5:16, Jer. 31:22, Ps. 97:12). Of course, there are commands to "do the right and the good" (Deut. 6:18), to "walk in His ways" (Deut. 28:9), and to use honest weights and measures (Lev. 19:36). But these themes are not used concomitantly with the idea of holiness.

In 1887, the first discovery was made of a collection of correspondence that would become known as the Amarna Letters. In the ensuing decades, nearly 400 more tablets or fragments were recovered, representing correspondence

79. There is a possible early equation of holiness with justice in the toponym Kadesh, which is identified as En-mishpat in Gen. 14:7. Snaith, for example, sees embryonic morality in the root *ḳ-d-sh* (1964: 32).

between Egypt and its neighbors, dated to the middle of the fourteenth century BCE. About 60 of the letters were written by Rib-Addi, King of Gubla (modern Byblos, Lebanon, about 50 miles north of Beirut), in correspondence Pharaoh Akhenaten (reigned c. 1353-1336 BCE), who is credited with introducing early monotheism to Egypt. In one letter, codified as Amarna Letter 137 (*EA* 137), Rib-Addi laments, "I personally am unable to enter the land of Egypt. I am old and there is a serious illness in my body. The king, my lord, knows that the gods of Gubla are holy [*qadišu*], and the pains are severe, for I committed sins against the gods." The conclusion is unchangeable and inescapable, and Rib-Addi can never be reconciled with the gods.

The biblical leader Joshua was an approximate contemporary of Akhenaten, and in his farewell address he appears to put forth a similar message: "you cannot worship the Lord, *because He is a holy God*; He is a jealous God who will not forgive your transgressions or your sins" (Josh. 24:19). This is not to suggest that Joshua was aware of—or sought to invert—Rib-Addi's message. More likely, the common idea existed in the ancient Near East that punishment was a result of God's holiness. However, this idea is employed in opposite ways. Rib-Addi accepts his fate and expresses little hope of salvation. Rib-Addi is reserved to his fate, while Joshua uses the idea of holiness to inspire repentance for the past and diligence in the future.

Contrasting with Rib-Addi, we can examine the Yehimilk Inscription, which is approximately four hundred years later (somewhere between the twelfth and tenth centuries), and takes a new different conception of holiness, directly connecting the idea of holiness with righteousness:

> This is the temple that Yehimilk king of Byblos rebuilt. He restored the ruins of these temples. May Baalshamem, the Mistress of Byblos, and the assembly of the holy gods prolong the days of Yehimilk and his years over Byblos, for he is a righteous [tz-d-ḳ] king and an upright [y-sh-r] king before the holy ones of Byblos.[80]

Even in surrounding cultures, holiness is paired with capriciousness (Rib-Addi) and justice (Yehimilk).

Snaith sees another shift with the eighth-century prophets that included Isaiah, Amos, and Hosea. Isaiah is the one prophet who explicitly linked holiness to justice when he wrote that God is *niḳdash bi-tzedakah*, "sanctified by righteousness" (Isa. 5:16). In Pentateuchal sources, God's being sanctified is a public display, so when Isaiah said, "sanctified by righteousness," there is a clear divergence from holiness as a grand observable event, to holiness being manifest through righteousness.[81] However, Isaiah's theory of holiness is complex. While Isaiah says God is "sanctified by righteousness," he also quotes the angelic vision "holy, holy, holy" (Isa. 6:3), which almost certainly focuses on holiness *qua* transcendence, rather than

---

80. This translation is pieced together from *ANET* 653 and Gibson 198.

81. The Hebrew words *tzedek* and *tzedakah* can also mean "justice" in a juridical sense. Even on this verse, *tzedakah* may refer to God executing judgment against the wicked (Radak).

holiness *qua* righteousness. And God's transcendence is also emphasized in, "To whom shall you compare Me and who shall I be compared to, says Kadosh" (Isa. 40:25).

Isaiah's conception of holiness is typified by three separate components. First, the idea of holiness as justice: "sanctified by righteousness" (Isa. 5:16). Second, the idea of God's absolute otherness: "holy, holy, holy" (Isa. 6:3); and "To whom shall you compare Me... says Kadosh" (Isa. 40:25). Third, God is not just Kadosh, the entirely other, but also the "Holy One of Israel" (e.g., Isa. 1:4), and Isaiah uses that phrase more than any other prophet and probably originated the term; this is not a description of God's otherness, but the relationship He has with Israel. To this extent Malbim writes, "Wherever in this book [Isaiah] it just says 'the Lord' [YHVH] it speaks about the aspect of Him as the One who creates the world, renews it, and guides it according to His desire, wisdom, and ability," while Kedosh Yisrael speaks of God's "aspect of the specific and wondrous matters which He performs for the sake of Israel" (on Isa. 1:4; see also *Kuzari* 4:3, quoted later). Thus there are two contradictory ideas that are resolved in the idea of holiness: God's holiness is both moral and transcendent, and God's holiness is both absolute (Kadosh) and relational (Kedosh Yisrael).

Jeremiah, whose prophetic career began less than a century after Isaiah's death, also combined the themes of holiness and righteousness, though in a somewhat roundabout locution: "May the Lord bless you, O habitation of justice [*tz-d-ḳ*] and mountain of holiness [*ḳ-d-sh*]" (Jer. 31:22). Breuer notes that in the prophetic future, Israel will desire an ideal laid down at the place of righteousness and the mountain of holiness (1988: 249); in other words, this is a prophecy that links the two concepts, and perhaps viewed them as overlapping.

Psalm 97, which is a composite of earlier biblical phrases, also connects holiness with justice: "Rejoice in the Lord, you righteous ones, and give thanks to His holy name" (Ps. 97:12; this verse itself is a portmanteau of two biblical phrases, Ps. 32:11 and 30:5). The significance of this combination is that the author of Psalm 97 took two common biblical themes, holiness and justice, and seamlessly fused the concepts, to say that those who are just should properly acknowledge God's holiness.

Holiness and Transcendence

If the previous section dealt with the rational element of biblical holiness, here it is proper to analyze God's transcendence, otherness, and unrelatability, embodied in the verse: "Holy, holy, holy is the Lord of hosts; the whole world is filled with His glory" (Isa. 6:3).[82]

It is possible to reduce this to two basic schools of interpretation. The first school views the phrase *ḳadosh ḳadosh ḳadosh* as a continuous clause with a single meaning. The second school views each *ḳadosh* as having a different referent.

The *Kuzari* writes, "Isaiah heard an endless 'holy, holy, holy,' which meant that God is too high, too exalted, too holy, and too pure for any impurity of the people in whose midst His light dwells to touch Him" (*Kuzari* 4:3). Rudolf Otto, too, understood the trisagion as part of the otherness of the *mysterium tremendum* (p. 17). Rabbi Soloveitchik writes

---

82. Among Christian sources, this phrasing is repeated at Rev. 4:8.

that this phrase "conveys the experience of the exaltedness of God, of His separateness and remoteness, His infinity and transcdence" (2003: 56). For all of these authors, the phrase *kadosh kadosh kadosh* has a single, superlative meaning.

Alternatively, each *kadosh* may bear a separate meaning, and this maximalist interpretation is taken by the Targum, Radak, and R. Bahya. The Targum interprets the first "holy" as the heavens, the second as the earth, and the third as all of time (this interpretation of the Targum is incorporated to the Jewish liturgy). Radak also takes a maximalist approach, but he says the first "holy" refers to the world of angels and souls, the second "holy" to planets and stars, and the third to this world, the world of man. The Targum includes the holiness of time, which Kimhi omits in his exegetical comments on this verse. R. Bahya ben Asher also takes a maximalist interpretation, "*Holy* in the lower world, *Holy* in the spheres, *Holy* in the realm of the angels." Bahya reverses the order, from earth to heaven, as opposed to Kimhi, who sees it as heaven to earth.

The following chart notes how each appearance of "holy" is interpreted:

	Targum	Kimhi	Bahya
First "holy"	Heaven	World of angels and souls	Lower world
Second "holy"	Earth	Planets and stars	Spheres
Third "holy"	Time	World of man	Angels

Holiness & Divine Wrath

> And all should cry, Beware! Beware!
> His flashing eyes, his floating hair!
> Weave a circle round him thrice,
> And close your eyes with holy dread,
> For he on honey-dew hath fed,
> And drunk the milk of Paradise.
>
> — Samuel Taylor Coleridge, "Kubla Kahn"

In several other places, the Bible expresses fear of approaching God, or limits those who can approach Him. For example: "O Lord, who can dwell in Your tent, and who can abide on Your holy mountain?" (Ps. 15:1; also Ps. 24:3). Briggs notes, "not what person, but what sort of person... among the accepted worshippers." (1906: 215). This Psalm, which was probably recited in ritual approach to the Temple, answers that only those of clean hands and pure hearts may enter. This idea is manifest in other faiths as well. The Quran states that "none shall touch it [the Quran] except the purified" (Quran 56:79). Some Muslims, taking this passage literally, actually proscribe certain people from touching the book.

From an Israelite perspective, this sentiment is not just a poetic ideal, but a legal requirement. Milgrom writes, "A deliberate, brazen sinner is barred from the sanctuary" (1991: 228). If someone touches or approaches God's place without permission, the results are often fatal, and there are at least five passages where there is risk of death or actual tragedy as a result of improper approach: the Israelites (Exod. 19:12), Nadab and

Abihu (Lev. 10:1-3), the Kohathites (Num. 4:19-20), the men of Beth-shemesh (1 Sam. 6:19), and Uzzah (2 Sam. 6:6-7). These examples stand in sharp contrast to Eleazar, "And the men of Kirjath-jearim came, and they brought up the Ark of the Lord, and brought it into the house of Abinadab on the hill and *k-d-sh*-ed Eleazar his son to guard the Ark of the Lord" (1 Sam. 7:1).[83]

Because the men of Kiriath-jearim sanctified him, Eleazar became a proper custodian for the ark. Milgrom thus writes, "'Holy' is thus aptly defined, in any context, as 'that which is unapproachable except through divinely imposed restriction,' or "that which is withdrawn from common use'" (1991: 730). Lasine quotes a series of metaphors of the destructive element of holiness. He quotes from Haran and Propp of a "lethal aura" and a "nuclear power plant," Knohl's "kind of minefield," Kaminsky's "electric charge," and Otto's "stored electricity" (2010: 35).

Perhaps this imagery of wrath can be understood much more simply. Earlier, we have shown that the verses link the idea of holiness with the idea of mitzvah-observance. The inverse is that if there is no mitzvah-observance, then the holiness is squandered or violated. That desecration of holiness, in the form of sin, might be what creates a state of danger in these instances.

Based on this fear, *k-d-sh* appears several times with *'-r-tz*, "tremble." For example, Isaiah criticizes: "with their mouths they have honored Me, but their hearts are far from Me" (Isa. 29:13). Isaiah condemns them, declaring, "When he sees his

83. The interpretations of *k-d-sh* in this verse parallel those of Exod. 19:10.

children, the work of My hands in his midst, they shall sanctify My name, the holy One of Jacob, and they shall tremble [*'-r-tz*] before the God of Israel" (Isa. 29:23; cf. Isa. 8:13).

The Sabbath *Amidah* builds on this verse, and serves as fulfillment of the prophet's words. Isaiah declares that there will be people in the future who sanctify and fear God. Jews, in reciting the *Ḳedushah*, declare that "we are the ones who sanctify and revere You," so every congregant who stands in communal prayer affirms that he will no longer engage in mechanical worship, as Isaiah criticized, but will renew his religious experience. Zimmels also quotes from R. Jacob b. Asher, author of the *Tur*, that Sephardim look downward when reciting the *Ḳedushah*, "while the children of Ashkenaz and Zarephath turn their eyes upward, raising their bodies" (1997: 111). This shows two responses to holiness: looking down in humility or skyward in inspiration.

The Wrath of Idolatry

God's wrath is especially fierce regarding idolatry. This is one of the most common themes of the Bible, and it relates intrinsically to holiness. Jeremiah declares, "And I shall sanctify destroyers against you... because they have abandoned the covenant of the Lord" (Jer. 22:7-9), and again "Sanctify nations against her, the Kings of Medes, its captains, officers, and the entire kingdom" (Jer. 51:28). The phrase *ḳ-d-sh milḥamah* is better translated, "sanctify [for] war," rather than "prepare for war." The sacral element in these passages is twofold: (1) there were rituals observed before going to battle, and (2) God acts for the sake of His holiness and His jealousy against idols.

God threatens to destroy Israel, but He also threatens to destroy Israel's oppressors, "Now I shall return the captives of Jacob and show mercy to the whole house of Israel, and I shall be jealous for My holy Name" (Ezek. 39:25). This passage inverts the theme. Instead of God's threatening to destroy Israel as sinners, He protects Israel and destroys her oppressors. God invokes His holiness to act for the sake of His holy nation. In all of these cases, however, God acts destructively for a purpose that is called holy.

Fire and Water

God's holiness is compared to fire, "And the Light of Israel shall be as a fire, and its Holy One as a flame and devour his thorns and brambles in one day" (Isa.10:17). Fire has the power for great good or great harm. God's fire is what inaugurated the altar (Lev. 9:24), but fire also slew Nadab and Abihu for their sin (Lev. 10:1-3).

God's holiness is also compared to consuming waters (Exod. 15:10-12). Water is associated with the primeval state of mankind. The Talmud implies that all the water in the world comes forth from the Euphrates, one of the rivers that flowed from primordial Eden (*Bekhorot* 55a-b). The fact that purification rites are aqueous is significant. Aryeh Kaplan comments that once the supplicant is purified, he is transformed and returned into his original state of perfection and sinlessness and "he is re-establishing his link with Eden" (1991b: 340).

From the beginning of religious practice, many religious rituals have required water. One Ugaritic text reads *b'l qdšm b nhr*, "Baal sanctified [purified?] them in the river" (Olmo Lete

2003). Ritual lavation is prescribed in Exod. 30:1-21, which uses the root *r-ḥ-tz*, "wash," four times, and Onkelos translates each one with the root *ḳ-d-sh*, "sanctify." Onkelos' reasoning is compelling. Since this water is required for the holy priests to permit them to enter a holy place, the water itself—as the medium to permit the priests' entrance—has a sanctifying property. Rashi notes that the Talmud also calls this process "sanctification [*ḳ-d-sh*] of the hands and feet" (*Zevaḥim* 19b).

A similar phenomenon appears in Psalms, "I wash [*r-ḥ-tz*] my hands in innocence, and may I go about Your altar, O Lord" (Ps. 26:6). Again, the Targum renders the biblical *r-ḥ-tz*, "wash," with the root *ḳ-d-sh*. But it is more a conceptual development than a linguistic one. Propp's analysis is persuasive: "the face, hands, and feet are the only skin not covered by the sacred vestments; thus they may need independent purification" (2006: 530). Anyone entering the Temple required ritual washing, which achieved holiness sufficient to grant that privilege.

The use of *r-ḥ-tz* in Ps. 26:6 deviates conceptually from the passage in Exod. 30:18-21. Psalm 26:6 says, "I will wash my hands *in innocence*," but not with water. Although the Psalmist invokes the imagery of Exodus 30, he is not refering to the precise rituals demanded in Exodus 30. Rabbi S.R. Hirsch explains: "A striving for purity, for blamelessness in one's dealings with one's fellow-men, is a prerequisite if one is to approach the Sanctuary and to join that group which is united around God's altar." Aristeas records that handwashing (in a river) before prayer is "witness that they had done no wrong, since the hands are the organs of all activity; in such beautiful and holy spirit do they make all things symbols of righteousness and truth" (305-306). Similarly, Ibn Ezra comments, "since all of [man's] actions are with the hands, the verse mentioned 'clean hands' [*naki kappayim*] for he has done nothing wrong" (on Ps. 24:4).

However, water is also a destructive element, and was the object of choice in the times of Noah. Like fire, the capacities of water are both for great advancement and for great calamnity.

The Sages later decreed that everyone should wash his hands when awaking. In doing so, they concretized the sentiment of Psalm 26, as Hirsch writes that the hands "so significantly [are] taken to represent the whole activity of Man, the purity of which depends on the morality of *every* sphere of his life" (on Lev. 15:33). The hands are an obvious synecdoche for man's action and involvement in the world. Their washing creates a psychological and existential state that one's actions should be directed in service to the Divine. R. Solomon b. Aderet, the Rashba, explains the institution of handwashing upon waking, "We are required to sanctify [*k-d-sh*] ourselves in His holiness and to wash our hands from a vessel [*keli*] like a priest who sanctifies [*k-d-sh*] his hands from the basin [*kiyyor*] before his service" (*Teshuvot ha-Rashba* 1:191). The Rashba is invoking the distinct imagery of Exodus 30. Where the priestly service is limited to the confines of the holy Temple, every Israelite is also called to holiness, but his region of work is the entire world, everything he touches, changes, alters, and has interaction with.[84]

---

84. However, the phrase "holy water" only appears once, regarding the *sotah* (rebellious wife – Num. 5:17), possibly because the water is sanctified in the firepan (Onkelos, Rashi, Ibn Ezra, Rashbam).

Punishment & Repentance

Gammie writes that holiness "is not simply punitive or retributive but above all purposive and purgative."[85] MacIntosh writes similarly, "Man punishes to destroy: God intervenes for the purpose of correction" (1997: 465). The purpose of destructive holiness is to purge the evil, not to punish it. God's punishment is meant to purge the subversive elements in society, in order to preserve order and observance on the whole. The analogy to amputation is frequently utilized here, where removing an atrophied limb preserves the remaining body. Another comparison is to a gardener who prunes a misplaced branch of a bush for the aesthetic sake of the whole. Similarly, the destructive and wanton sinner puts everyone around him at risk.

The three acts of repentance, prayer, and charity were all tied back to the original notion of sacrifices, and all create a status of purity and atonement. Repentance (specifically, confession) is a biblically mandated component of bringing an offering (Lev. 5:5, Num. 5:6), which Maimonides emphasizes (*Teshuvah* 1:3-4). Prayer stretches back at least to Abraham, and is sometimes used as a proxy for sacrifices both in the Bible and Talmud (Ps. 141:2, Hos. 14:1-2, *Berakhot* 26b). Charity exists in the Pentateuch (e.g., Deut. 15:7-11), but its penitential aspect does not appear until the Second Temple (Dan. 4:24, Sir. 3:30), and charity itself takes on the role of sacrifices in the Talmud (*Menaḥot* 97a). The Sages taught that the three acts

---

85. Gammie 1989: 89. Gammie is refering specifically to holiness in the book of Isaiah, but his notion can be easily extended to the rest of the Hebrew Bible. Note the use of *kadosh* in Isa. 4:3, which is after *tzemaḥ YHVH*, which according to Targum and Radak is Messiah; hence those who remain after the messianic wars are called "holy."

of reprentance, prayer, and charity can achieve a purity of the soul. And since purity is a prerequisite for holiness, these acts allow the repentant sinner to stand in the presence of God.

Eschatological Holiness

Implicit in these verses is not just a call for the three righteous acts of repentance, prayer, and charity, which avert the evil decree. There is also a concept of the eschaton, the end of days, the final order of things. The prophet Zechariah declares, "On that day there shall be on the bells of the horses, 'Holy to the Lord,' and the pots of of house of the Lord shall be like the receptacles before the altar. And every pot in Jerusalem and Judah shall be holy to the Lord, the Lord of Hosts..." (Zech. 14:20-21, cf. Isa. 66:7). The phrase "holy to the Lord" appears only here and at Exod. 28:36, 39:30. In Exodus, it designates the High Priest, while in the book of Zechariah, it refers to everything that exists on earth. The root k-d-sh has the semantic component "separated," so the difficulty with this passage is that it suggests everything will be holy. But if everything is separated, nothing is separated; and if everything is holy, then nothing is holy.

Zechariah, however, is discussing an eschatological holiness. Meyers and Meyers write, "the eschatological age will involve a reversal of temporal reality, with its distinctions between sacred and profane" (1998: 480). In the eschaton, everything that remains will have survived the consuming fire (however one understands that term); it will be the "remaining ones" that will be "separated" from everything else that has already been destroyed, and thus everything remaining will be holy. Eschatological holiness is fundamentally different than terrestrial this-wordly holiness.[86] Cheyne wrote, "Whatever interferes with His supreme right of property in Israel, He must destroy, but He will not so chastise His chosen people as to extinguish it all together. All that will be left will be holy..." (1884: 111).[87]

Thus there is a clear development from Rib-Addi, through to the prophecies of Isaiah, Jeremiah, and Ezekiel, that holiness has a destructive element. This culminates in Zechariah's eschatological vision that all will be destroyed except that which is worthy to survive—that which is holy.

---

86. This interpretation is not following the Talmud, which states that things will be holy only as far as a horse can run in half a day (*Pesaḥim* 50a).

87. I hope to write a tract on theodicy, the problem of evil. I am venturing into the problem of evil in this study only insofar as it might relate to the idea of holiness.

Chapter 8

Hellenistic Holiness

Then we must begin again and ask. What is piety?
That is an enquiry which I shall never be weary of pursuing.

— Socrates

Euthyphro

Perhaps the earliest philosophical analysis of holiness, in any civilization, is Socrates' *Euthyphro*. The dialogue revolves around a man named Euthyphro, who has brought charges against his father for killing a servant. Euthyphro laments that he is being criticized: "a son is impious who prosecutes his father. Which shows, Socrates writes, how little they know what the gods think about piety and impiety." This gives Socrates an opening to enquire how Euthyphro defines the terms.

Euthyphro's first reply is as follows: "Piety is doing as I am doing; that is to say, prosecuting anyone who is guilty of murder, sacrilege, or of any similar crime—whether he be your father or mother, or whoever he may be—that makes no difference; and not to prosecute them is impiety." Socrates replies that this may be an example of piety, but he counters, "Remember that I did not ask you to give me two or three examples of piety, but to explain the general idea which makes all pious things pious." Socrates is requesting a unifying principle that connects all pious things.

Euthyphro offers a second attempt: "Piety, then, is that which is dear to the gods, and impiety is that which is not dear to them." This is a categorical answer, rather than an answer in the form of a list of examples. Socrates' reply to this is an appeal to the existence of a pantheon of gods, who often disagree with each other, and what is beloved to one god may be hated by another. As such, there will be some objects that are beloved by some gods and hated by others. Socrates, however, concedes that there may be some things that are universally beloved and other things that are universally reviled; and that things universally cherished may be regarded as pious and holy, while things universally despised are impious.

At this point, Socrates asks one of the most famous questions of the dialogue, "The point which I should first wish to understand is whether the pious or holy is beloved by the gods because it is holy, or holy because it is beloved of the gods." Euthyphro vascillates between these two options, and Socrates criticizes either conclusion. Either one is "an attribute only, and not the essence—the attribute of being loved by all the gods. But you still refuse to explain to me the nature of holiness."

Euthyphro's third answer is, "Piety or holiness, Socrates, appears to me to be that part of justice which attends to the gods, as there is the other part of justice which attends to men."

Socrates gives the reply, "And does piety or holiness, which has been defined [by you] to be the art of attending to the gods, benefit or improve them? Would you say that when you do a holy act you make any of the gods better?" Although not made explicit, it seems that both speakers agree that human beings cannot "make any of the gods better."

Euthyphro's fourth answer is to redefine "attends to the gods," and in doing so he now claims piety means, "as servants show their masters." He even concurs with Socrates' characterization as "a sort of ministration." Pushed further, Euthyphro says that "piety or holiness is learning how to please the gods in word and deed, by prayers and sacrifices." Socrates then traps Euthyphro that this ministration is also a form of benefitting the gods, which Euthyphro has already admitted is impossible because man cannot benefit the gods.

There are four explanations of piety or holiness in *Euthyphro*. First, Euthyphro says piety is prosecuting crime, regardless of the perpetrator. Socrates objects that this is an example of piety, not a definition. Second, Euthyphro says that which is holy is that which is beloved of the gods. Socrates counters that since gods can disagree, that cannot be a universal definition of the attribute of holiness. An important tangent asks whether holiness derives from the gods' love, or if the gods love things because of their inherent holiness. Then Euthyphro gives two definitions of holiness as "attending to the gods." The first definition is "that part of just which is attending to the gods" (which is his third overall definition of holiness) is a way to improve them. But Euthyphro and Socrates both reject the possibility of man having the influence to improve the gods. The fourth and final definition offered is the "attending to the gods" and learning "how to please the gods," which they both agree is not an inherent definition of holiness. Thus Socrates departs his conversant disappointed that he has not been supplied with a comprehensive essential definition of holiness and piety. The arguments can be presented in the chart to the right.

Protagoras

Socrates also discussed holiness in *Protagoras* (329-331). Protagoras concedes that justice, temperance, and holiness are all parts of virtue, much like the mouth, nose, eyes, and ears are all parts of the face.[88] Socrates tries to argue that "justice is either the same with holiness, or very nearly the same; and... that justice is like holiness and holiness is like justice." However, Protagoras refuses this final point, regardless of how Socrates entreats him.

Wakefield sees two possible ways to interpret Socrates' assertion:

(a) Justice and holiness are alike in themselves;
(b) Justice and holiness are alike in their powers (1987: 270).

Premise (a) essentially asserts that they are synonyms or nearly synonyms (a claim that has been examined earlier). Premise (b)

---

88. Levine, in the introduction to his commentary on *Leviticus*, writes, "Justice and compassion, too, were a dimension of holiness" (Levine 1989: xi). Levine is suggesting that justice and compassion are subsumed under holiness. Protagoras said that justice and holiness are not the same, but are both subsumed under *virtue*, while Socrates will argue that justice and holiness are the same or very nearly the same.

Euthyphro's Theories of Holiness		
	Euthyphro's Theory	Socrates' Objection
1	"Piety is doing as I am doing; that is to say, prosecuting anyone who is guilty of murder, sacrilege, or of any similar crime—whether he be your father or mother, or whoever he may be—that makes no difference; and not to prosecute them is impiety"	"I did not ask you to give me two or three examples of piety, but to explain the general idea which makes all pious things pious"
2	"Piety, then, is that which is dear to the gods, and impiety is that which is not dear to them"	There is a pantheon of gods, and they hold different things as dear
3	"Piety or holiness, Socrates, appears to me to be that part of justice which attends to the gods, as there is the other part of justice which attends to men."	"And does piety or holiness, which has been defined [by you] to be the art of attending to the gods, benefit or improve them? Would you say that when you do a holy act you make any of the gods better?"
4	"piety or holiness is learning how to please the gods in word and deed, by prayers and sacrifices."	Man cannot benefit the gods

goes in a different direction. Wakefield redefines (b) as making two claims that seem banal: First, "The power of Holiness is to produce holy acts." Second, "The power of Justice is to produce just acts" (1987: 274). Wakefield thus argues that holiness also has the power to produce acts of justice, and justice has the power to produce acts of holiness; hence Socrates' conclusion "that justice is either the same with holiness, or very nearly the same; and above all I would assert that justice is like holiness and holiness is like justice" (*Protagoras* 331). Wakefield sees this as an assertion of Premises (b) and then (a), above.

The Source of Holiness in Greek and Biblical Thought

Socrates posed the question, "The point which I should first wish to understand is whether the pious or holy is beloved by the gods because it is holy, or holy because it is beloved of the gods." Perhaps Socrates is inquirying about which quality is primary: holiness or godliness. Godliness is easier to understand, as it is that which directly relates to God or the gods. However if there is a separate, independent quale or status of holiness, then that attribute of holiness might be more primary than the attribute of godliness. As will be demonstrated in the section on Rabbi Judah Halevi, there is no question that Judaism believes that holiness is dependent on God, not the other way around.

Holiness and Justice in Greek and Biblical Thought

More than Semitic sources, these two Socratic dialogues—*Euthyphro* and *Protagoras*—fused the idea of holiness and justice. Aristeas also accepts this linkage, but in doing so, he also accepts the biblical rules of holiness and impurity.

Specifically, in explaining the laws of impurity and the dietary laws, Aristeas writes, "Do no accept the exploded idea that it was out of regard for 'mice' and 'weasel' and other such creatures that Moses ordained these laws with such scrupulous care; not so, these laws have all been solemnly drawn up for the sake of justice, to promote holy contemplation and the perfecting of character." He then explains that the permitted animals "are gentle and distinguished by cleanliness" while the forbidden creatures "are wild and carnivorous and with their strength oppress the rest and procue their food with injustice" (144-146). In the Torah, the dietary laws are about holiness, but for Aristeas, the dietary laws are about holiness *and* justice.

Philo of Alexandria, who flourished about two centuries after Aristeas, adopts many Socratic theories of holiness as virtue, while also applying them to biblical principles. He draws an idea almost straight from *Euthyphro*: "But it is not proper to call piety, which consists in ministering to God, a virtue which is conversant about supplying the things which will be of use to the Deity; for the Deity is not benefited by any one, inasmuch as He is not in need of anything" (*Worse* 55).

The four cardinal Greek virtues are temperance, courage, prudence, and justice. By contrast, the Bible has no explicit notion of "temperance," which in Greek thought is also related to ideas of moderation and restraint. Rather, the Bible uses ideas of separation (*perishut, havdalah*), and wisdom (*hokhmah*), commandedness (*mitzvah, tzivvui*) and of course holiness (*kedushah*). Philo was probably the first figure to systematically attempt an integration of the biblical and Greek traditions, which makes his legacy enduring and invaluable. In one passage he writes, "We have spoken before[89] of that queen of all the virtues, piety and holiness, and also of prudence and moderation; we must now proceed to speak of justice which is conversant about subjects which are akin and nearly related to them" (*Laws* IV.135). While Socrates said holiness and justice were at the same level, Philo elevated holiness as the "queen of all virtues."[90] Sterling adds, "Piety is for Philo, the virtue *par excellence* in which the other virtues are subsumed" (2006: 109).

Philo might also be the earliest source to connect holiness with the concept of *imitatio Dei*, saying that the holiness of resting on the Sabbath teaches, "Always imitate God; let that one period of seven days, in which God created the world, be to you a complete example of the way in which you are to obey the law" (*Decalogue* 100). Furthermore, Philo also takes a negative view of corporeality in general, believing that the bodily desires distract one from philosophical pursuits. Therefore he takes an ascetic position and advocates for withdrawal and renunciation of the physical world in order to achieve intellectual and philosophical accomplishments.

---

89. Whatever Philo is referring to here has been lost.
90. "In *Spec.* 4.135, we find a different definition of the four cardinal virtues: *eusebeia* (piety, sanctity) is defined as 'the queen of virtues,' and wisdom, temperance, and justice following" — *Stanford Encyclopedia of Philosophy*, "Philo of Alexandria" (accessed July 31, 2018).

Chapter 9

Talmudic Holiness

The objects regarded as sacred may differ from country to country, yet sensitivity to the sacred is universal.

— Abraham Joshua Heschel[91]

With the destruction of the Temple, the Israelite religion was forced to reorient itself. Sacrifices were no longer offered, and it was no longer necessary or even possible to observe many of the laws of ritual purity. As we have seen, purity is a prerequisite for holiness. But holiness was intimately connected with sacrifice; if offerings were (temporarily) discontinued, then most of the laws of purity lost their force.[92] After the destruction of the most sacred structure, the Israelites would adapt their faith in such a way that it remained relevant to the sage and commoner alike, which no doubt contributed to a shifting understanding of holiness. Concommitantly, they were

---

91. Heschel 1965: 48.
92. Some observances of purity still remain in effect, such as *niddah*, priests not entering a cemetery, and the controversy about ascending the Temple Mount.

also exposed to Greek philosophy, and while the faithful nation rejected some ideas as inconsistent and antithetical to central Jewish teaching, other ideas were judged acceptable and were absorbed either intentionally or osmotically.

In such a world, two themes became interwoven: holiness and virtue. Virtue is a quest for the excellent, and holiness stands in a relation to the Godly, so it is not surprising that these concepts should have been interwoven. Greek philosophy also advocates renunciation of the physical, as Aristotle said that the feeling of touch is "shameful." No verse in the Hebrew Bible explicitly advocates asceticism as a quality of holiness. Earlier, it was argued that biblical holiness entailed adherence to the commandments, either in their entirety, or a specific subset (dietary laws, sexual laws, idolatry). Exilic Judaism did in some places preseverve the notion that holiness is synonymous with mitzvah-observance, but in other places that epoch witnessed the term "holy" acquire a possible meaning of asceticism or supererogation as well.

Holiness *qua* mitzvah-observance is advocated in the following two rabbinic sources:

- When Scripture says "be holy," this refers to the holiness of all commandments (*Sifra* "Ḳedoshim" 10:2; quoted also in Maimonides, *Guide* 3:47).
- R. Joseph recited, "Read not *miḳdashi* [My Sanctuary] but *meḳuddashai* [My sanctified ones]." This refers to the people who fulfilled the Torah from *alef* to *tav* (*Shabbat* 55a, *Avodah Zarah* 4a).

Holiness as mitzvah-observance is the baseline, both in the Bible and in rabbinic literature. However, in rabbinic literature, there is an additional component of supererogation—of additional abstentions in pursuit of holiness.

"Sanctify Yourself with What is Permitted to You" (*Yevamot* 20a)

Some talmudic sources connect holiness with supererogation or asceticism. One talmudic passage teaches: "sanctify yourself with what is permitted to you" (*Yevamot* 20a). First, we must analyze the context where this statement appears:

> MISHNAH: The Sages said a general rule [in respect of the deceased brother's wife]: wherever she is prohibited as a forbidden relative, she may neither perform *halitzah* nor be taken in levirate marriage. If she is prohibited by a commandment or by holiness, she must perform *halitzah* and may not be taken in levirate marriage. If her sister is also her sister-in-law, she may perform *halitzah* or may be taken in levirate marriage. "Prohibited by a commandment" [refers to] the secondary relationships forbidden by the Sages. "Prohibited by holiness" [refers to the following forbidden categories]: a widow to a High Priest; a divorcee or one that had performed *halitzah* to an ordinary priest; a *mamzeret* or a *netinah* to an Israelite, and a daughter of an Israelite, to a *natin* or a bastard.

This Mishnah identifies three categories. The general category refers to the standard, though highly complex, relationships of the sixteen categories of women and how that relates to levirate marriage and *halitzah*. The second category is "prohibited by a commandment," and that refers to legislation whose origin is rabbinic, not biblical. The third category, "prohibited by holiness" refers to the rank of the individuals involved. The Talmud seeks to identify the parameters of these three categories. However, the following excerpt omits the discussion of the first category, the "general rule," and focuses on how the Talmud understands the final two categories, "prohibited by a commandment" and "prohibited by holiness."

> GEMARA: "Prohibited by a commandment" [refers to] the secondary relationships forbidden by the Sages. Why are these called "prohibited by a commandment"? Abbaye said: Because it is a commandment to follow the words of the Sages.
>
> "Prohibited by holiness" [refers to the following forbidden categories]: a widow to a High Priest; a divorcee or one that had performed *halitzah* to an ordinary priest. Why are these called "prohibited by holiness"? Because it is written, "They [i.e., the priests] shall be holy to their God" (Lev. 21:6).
>
> It was taught: R. Judah reverses the order: "Prohibited by a commandment" [refers to the following prohibited categories]: a widow to a High Priest; a divorcee or one that had performed *halitzah* to an ordinary priest. And why are these called "prohibited by

a commandment"? Because it is written, "These are the commandments" (Lev. 27:34). "Prohibited by holiness" [refers to] the secondary relationships forbidden by the Sages. And why are these called "prohibited by virtue of holiness"? Abbaye said: Because whoever heeds the words of the Sages is called holy. Rava then said to him: Then whoever does not fulfill the words of the Sages is called neither holy nor wicked? Rather, Rava said, "Sanctify yourself by what is permitted to you" (*Yevamot* 20a).

The chart on the next page indicates how the two talmudic opinions understand the terms "prohibited by a commandment" and "prohibited by holiness."

From a legal perspective, both categories—"prohibited by a commandment" and "prohibited by holiness"—have the same practical ramification, i.e., *halitzah* is required because she is ineligible for levirate marriage.

From a theological perspective, however, the difference of rationales is of great consequence. Rava's position, once limited to a question of who is ineligible for levirate marriage, became one of the most famous statements concerning holiness. This passage shows the transition of holiness from mitzvah-observance to supererogation. Nahmanides expanded the scope even further, as this phrase became the cornerstone of his theory of holiness.[93]

---

93. The theory of Nahmanides will be discussed later. The focus of this chapter is how the Talmud and rabbinic literature, not the Medievals, treated the idea of holiness.

Yevamot 20a

	First Opinion (Anonymous)	Rationale:	Second Opinion (Rabbi Judah)	Rationale:
Prohibited by a commandment	Rabbinic Legislation	Abbaye: It is a commandment to follow the words of the Sages.	Caste Restrictions	It is written: "These are the commandments" (Lev. 27:34)
Prohibited by holiness	Caste Restrictions	It is written (of the priests): "They shall be holy to their God"	Rabbinic Legislation	Abbaye: Whoever heeds the words of the Sages is called holy. Rava: Sanctify yourself in what is permitted to you.

Sciatic Nerve (*Ḥullin* 91a)

Another case of talmudic supererogation regards the consumption of the sciatic nerve (*gid ha-nasheh*). The Talmud analyzes the parameters of the restriction and concludes, "its fat is permitted, but the Israelites are holy [*Yisra'el kedoshim*] and acted as if it were forbidden" (*Ḥullin* 91a, 92b). Rashi says this is a "fence around the Torah," which suggests Rashi might equate "the Israelites are holy" with rabbinic legislation. Alternatively, Ritva (Rabbi Yom Tov ben Abraham Aseville) suggests the phrase "the Israelites are holy" refers to a popular, layman's campaign to treat the fat of the sciatic nerve as prohibited (s.v. *Rav Asi*). Whether one takes a top-down approach (Rashi) or a bottom-up approach (Ritva), the practice from talmudic times onward has been to abstain from this fat though it is technically permitted. And this abstention is done in the name of holiness.

Ḳodesh Hillulim (Lev. 19:24, *Berakhot* 35a)

Another unique example of talmudic holiness concerns the phrase *kodesh hillulim la-YHVH* (loosely, "a sacred offering of praise to God" – Lev. 19:24). The first three years of a tree's growth is considered *orlah*, and prohibited to be eaten at all. The fourth year is one of transition, since those fruits must be brought to Jerusalem and eaten there, and that is called *kodesh hillulim la-YHVH*. The Talmud puns on the words *hillulim* ("praises") as *ḥillulim* ("desanctified objects"), from which it derives the obligation to render a blessing before and after eating—once before and once after since *hillulim* is plural (*Berakhot* 35a). The original context is specifically about the desacralization procedure of the fourth-year fruit, but the

Talmud expands the context to food in general, regardless of the type of food or when it was grown. In this model, anything that grows—not just fourth-year fruit—is holy, and is in God's domain, and man can only desacralize and use it after reciting a blessing over it, thereby drawing it into the sphere of the mundane.

The blessing makes the food fit for ordinary use. Thus the Talmud states, "It is forbidden for anyone to derive pleasure from this world without [rendering] a blessing. And anyone who benefits from this world without a benediction has committed sacrilege [m-'-l]."[94] The Talmud extends this to—quite literally—anything in the world, suggesting that even common objects are holy to the Lord until someone renders a blessing to desanctify it and permit it for human use. This talmudic passage later quotes, "The earth is the Lord's and the fullness thereof" (Ps. 24:1), creating a parallel between the Temple and the world, since me'ilah, which biblically applies only to Temple property, now applies to ordinary foodstuffs. As Rashi comments: "'committed sacrilege' — as if he benefitted from holy objects." Where biblical me'ilah is a strictly defined offense against Temple property, this talmudic, metaphorical me'ilah encompasses everything in the world.[95]

---

94. The biblical idea of me'ilah has already been addressed; here we show the talmudic application.

95. Another case of of supererogation is, "Rabbi Zeira said: The daughters of Israel are stringent upon themselves, for even if they see a drop of [menstrual] blood the size of a mustard seed, they observe seven clean days" (Megillah 28b). Both Rashi and Maimonides (Issurei Biah 11:4) say this practice is because of a doubt as to whether she has the status of a niddah or a zavah. It is speculative but possible that specifically because this law relates to sexual intimacy, the stringency emerged in this case.

Imitatio Dei (*Shabbat* 133b)

The idea of *imitatio Dei* ("imitating God") is presented as one of the main interpretations of holiness,[96] and perhaps one of the central tenets of Judaism in general. Some candidate verses to confirm this theory include:

- "God created man in his image" (Gen. 1:27).
- "You shall be holy, for I the Lord your God am holy" (Lev. 19:2).
- "The Lord your God you shall follow" (Deut. 13:5).
- "The Lord will establish you as His holy people, as he has sworn to you, if you keep the commandments of the Lord your God and walk in His ways" (Deut 28:9).

Seforno, for example, links together the idea of "let us make man in our image according to our likeness" (Gen. 1:26) and "You shall be holy" (Lev. 19:2), saying "to be as similar as possible to their Creator" (on Lev. 19:2).

Nonetheless, in Tanakh the relationship between man and God is never one of mimesis or emulation. The Bible uses many analogies to describe the relationship between God and man: father/son, master/slave, husband/wife, friend, lover, shepherd, farmer, and vineyard, but not one of mimesis. In the Garden of Eden, the serpent entices the primordial woman, "For God

---

96. Two prominent Bible scholars have suggested the idea of *imitatio dei* is present in the Bible. Jacob Milgrom writes, "The reason that Israel must aspire to holiness is *imitatio dei*" (1991: 687; 2000: 1605). William Propp, comparing Exod. 13:2 and Num. 3:12-13, suggests several resolutions, including, "one might say that [Exod.] 13:2 commands *imitatio dei*, sanctifying what [God] has already made holy."

knows that when you eat of it your eyes will be opened, and you will be like God,[97] knowing good and evil" (Gen. 3:5). This temptation to "be like God," and eating the forbidden fruit, created a tragic end for man's stay in Eden.

The rejection of *imiatio Dei* is also present in the story of the tower of Babel: "Come, let us build ourselves a city, and a tower with its top in the heavens, and let us make a name for ourselves" (Gen. 11:4), which the commentaries understand as wanting to be as high as God. Again, the consequences are tragic: man is dispersed throughout the land and his language is confounded.[98] Third, the book of Isaiah reads: "To whom shall you compare Me and who shall I be compared to, says Kadosh [the Holy One]" (40:25). God, specifically in His quale of holiness, is emphasized as incomparable.

Nonetheless, several rabbinic passages appear to endorse *imitatio Dei*:

- Abba Saul said *ve-anvehu* means I will be like Him [*ani ve-Hu*]: Just as He is gracious and compassionate, so you must be gracious and compassionate (*Shabbat* 133b).

---

97. Hebrew, *Elohim*. See however Onkelos and Maimonides (*Guide* 1:2).

98. There are ancient sources that mention the idea of imitating God or the gods. In Ugaritic literature, when Baal died, his sister Anat and the goddess Shapshu lamented him "in imitation of the supreme god" (Del Olmo Lete 1999: 161, quoting *KTU* I.6 I 17-18, cf. *Sotah* 14a). Anthropologically, see Durkheim 1915: 396. Socrates says, "we ought to fly away from earth to heaven as quickly as we can; and to fly away is to become like God, as far as possibly; and to become like him is to become holy, just, and wise" (*Theaetetus* 176). See also Philo, *Decalogue* 100, Matt. 5:48, Luke 6:36, and Ephes. 5:1.

- R. Hama son of R. Hanina further said: … walk after the attributes of the Holy One, blessed be He. As He clothes the naked… so do you also clothe the naked. The Holy One, blessed be He, visited the sick… so do you also visit the sick. The Holy One, blessed be He, comforted mourners… so do you also comfort mourners. The Holy one, blessed be He, buried the dead… so do you also bury the dead (*Sotah* 14a; see also Maimonides, *De'ot* 1:6).

Despite these sources, I am not convinced that *imitatio Dei* is a central Jewish concept. For example, the phrase "walking in God's ways" (Deut. 28:9) is traditionally understood to mean *walk in the ways which God behaves*. However, the verse can be read, more simply: *walk in the ways that He instructs us to behave.*[99]

Some of those instructions will overlap with ways in which God is said to behave, but God also has brought plagues and earthquakes—calamities man is not expected to effectuate. The relationship between God and man is a complex topic in Tanakh, but many of the metaphors are reciprocal: husband and wife have reciprocal responsibilities, as do father and son. The overlapping of responsibilities does not demonstrate identical tasks, but speaks to the idea of covenant. For example, "Now therefore, if you obey My voice and keep My covenant… [you

---

99. The context here is important: "The Lord will establish you as His holy people, as He has sworn to you, if you keep the commandments of the Lord your God and walk in His ways." Here "walking in His ways" is paralleled with "keeping the commandments." In fact Ibn Ezra is of the opinion that "walking in His ways" means nothing more than "keeping the commandments."

shall be] a holy nation" (Exod. 19:5-6). Rashi understands "covenant" here as a reference to the Torah; i.e., the Torah that is being revealed at that moment.[100] There is also a reference to a "holy covenant" at Dan. 11:28, which *Metzudat David* says is a reference to the Torah.

Extending the idea further, a covenant is a contract, and one can view such an agreement with either lethargy or alacrity—one can meet the bare minimum expectation or one can be eager and animated out of affection for the other party. This idea is certainly closer to *devekut* than *imitatio Dei*. It is extraordinarily dangerous when man engages in self-deification. Rather, the relationship between man and God should follow one of these other models of reciprocality, rather that mimesis.

However, if we are forced to concede that *imitatio Dei* is a bona fide Jewish idea, then we must add two caveats. First, *imitatio Dei* is a principle that applies when there is no other law that applies, in the way that concepts like *kedoshim tihyu* or *ve-asita ha-yashar ve-ha-tov*, "and you shall do the right and the good" (Deut. 6:18) fill in the missing pieces. Nahmanides famously says that the Torah could not address every possibility, and therefore God gave general rules in such circumstances. We should not elevate *imitatio Dei* to an overarching principle of actional obligation, but only use it when there is not a specific law that can be applied.[101]

---

100. Nahmanides however understands it as the covenant that God made with the Patriarchs.
101. Wright however apparently tries to split the difference: "The people, too, are charged to emulate God's holiness by keeping the commandments" (1992: 238).

Second, under no circumstances should we say that *imitatio Dei* is a dispensation to bring earthquakes, floods, and other disasters. Rather, *imitatio Dei* should be understood narrowly. For example, Aristeas understood it as "imitating the gentleness of God" (*Aristeas* 188). The forces other than kindness are not for us to mimic in pursuit of *imitatio Dei*.

Rabbi Pinhas ben Yair

Rabbi Pinhas ben Yair was a second-century CE Tanna, and he authored a passage that uses many of the terms that we have discussed so far (such as *perishut*, *taharah*, and *kedushah*), and since he does so systematically, it allows us to ascertain the differences between the terms. However, there are some problems because there are variances between the two handwritten manuscripts of the Mishnah (Kaufmann and Parma codices), and in the printed versions (e.g., at M. *Sotah* 9:15, BT *Avodah Zarah* 20b, JT *Shekalim* 9b; there is also version that underlaid what Maimonides wrote at *Tum'at Okhalin* 16:14). The different versions are presented in a chart on the next page.

Most versions have the order *perishut* → *taharah* → *kedushah* → *hasidut* (sometimes with intervening attributes), and there is no reason to think that any of these terms are synonymous, since each quality is said to bring about the next one in the progression. It must be emphasized that R. Pinhas b. Yair saw each term as a discrete concept, thus he did not view *perishut* as synonymous with *kedushah*. The progression being taught and emphasized: "separation" can be any type of separation; "purity" means freedom from a contaminant, or

Kaufmann (with marginal notes in brackets)	
Printed Mishnah (Kehati)	
Yerushalmi Printed (*Shekalim* 9b)	
Bavli (*Avodah Zarah* 20b JTS)	
Bavli (*Avodah Zarah* 20b Paris)	
Bavli (*Avodah Zarah* 20b with interpolations from marginal note)	

ר' פינחס בן יאיר או' זריזות מביאה לידי נקיות נקיות לידי [פרישות פרישות לידי] טהרה טהרה לידי קדושה קדושה לידי ענווה ענוה לידי יראת חטא [יראת חטא לידי] חסידות חסידות לידי רוח ה' הקודש רוח הקודש לידי תחיית המתים באה לידי אליהו זכור לטוב
רבי פנחס בן יאיר אומר זריזות מביאה לידי נקיות ונקיות מביאה לידי טהרה וטהרה מביאה לידי פרישות ופרישות מביאה לידי קדושה וקדושה מביאה לידי ענוה וענוה מביאה לידי יראת חטא ויראת חטא מביאה לידי חסידות וחסידות מביאה לידי רוח הקדש ורוח הקדש מביאה לידי תחיית מתים ותחיית המתים באה על ידי אליהו זכור לטוב אמן
היה רבי פינחס בן יאיר אומר זריזות מביאה לידי נקיות נקיות מביאה לידי טהרה טהרה מביאה לידי קדושה קדושה מביאה לידי ענוה ענוה מביאה לידי יראת חטא מביאה לידי חסידות חסידות מביאה לידי רוח הקודש רוח הקודש מביאה לידי תחיית המתים תה''מ מביאה לידי אליהו הנביא זכור לטוב
אמר ר' פינחס בן יאיר זהירות מביאה לידי זריזות זריזות מביאה לידי נקיות נקיות מביאה לידי פרישות פרישות מביאה לידי טהרה טהרה מביאה לידי קדושה מביאה לידי יראת חטא יראת חטא מביאה לידי ענוה ענוה מביאה לידי חסידות חסידו' גדולה מכולן שנ' אז דברת בחזון חסידיך ופליגא דר' יהושע בן לוי ענוה גדולה מכלן שנ' רוח ה' אלקים עלי יען משח ה' אלקים אותי לבשר ענוים לבשר חסידי' לא נאמר אלא לבשר ענוים הרי למדת שענוה גדולה מכלן
אמר פינחס בן יאיר זהירות מביאה לידי זריזות זריזות מביאה לידי נקיות נקיות מביאה לידי פרישות פרישות מביאה לידי טהרה טהרה מביאה לידי קדושה קדושה מביאה לידי יראת חטא יראת חטא מביאה לידי ענוה ענוה מביאה לידי חסידות חסידות גדולה מכו־לם שנ' אז דברתא בחזון חסידיך ופליגא דר' יהושע בן לוי דאמר יהושע בן לוי ענוה גדולה מכולם שנ' רוח ה' אלקים עלי יען משח ה' אותי לבשר ענוים לבשר חסידים וצדיקים לא נאמר אלא ענוים הא למדת שענוה גדולה מכולן
א''ר פנחס בן יאיר תורה מביאה לידי זהירות זהירות מביאה לידי זריזות זריזות מביאה לידי נקיות נקיות מביאה לידי פרישות פרישות מביאה לידי טהרה טהרה מביאה לידי קדושה קדושה מביאה לידי ענוה ענוה מביאה לידי יראת חטא יראת חטא מביאה לידי חסידות חסידות מביאה לידי רוח רוח הקודש רוח הקודש מביאה לידי תחיית המתים וחסידות גדולה מכולן ופליגא דר' יהושע בן לוי דא''ר יהושע בן לוי ענוה גדולה מכולן שנאמר רוח ה' אלקים עלי יען משח ה' אותי לבשר ענוים חסידים לא נאמר אלא ענוים הא למדת שענוה גדולה מכולן

"adequately segregated"[102]; "holiness" is a positive concept, a greater and more profound connection with the divine. To this extent, Harvey writes, "Distinctions in nature are perceived by *homo sapiens*, distinctions in holiness by *homo religiosus*" (1977: 13). The culmination of this process is personal piety. In rabbinic writings, *hasidut*, meaning, "piety, saintliness," frequently means "superholiness" or "extra-holiness."

Since this dictum appears in multiple places, many different authorities composed commentaries on this passage. First we can look at the version as it appears in the Bavli. The Bavli's text (corrected in accordance with the marginal note and the manuscript versions) reads:

> R. Pinhas b. Yair said: Study [*Torah*] leads to caution [*zehirut*], caution leads to zeal [*zerizut*], zeal leads to cleanliness [*neki'ut*], cleanliness leads to separation [*perishut*], separation leads to purity [*taharah*], purity leads to holiness [*kedushah*], holiness leads to humility [*anavah*], humility leads to fear of sin [*yir'at het*], fear of sin leads to piety [*hasidut*], saintliness leads to the [possession of] the holy spirit [*ruah ha-kodesh*], the holy spirit leads to resurrection of the dead [*tehiyyat ha-metim*]. And piety is greater than any of these, for Scripture says, "Then you did speak in a vision to Your pious ones [*hasidekha*]" (Ps. 89:20) (*Avodah Zarah* 20b).

---

102. Milgrom 2000: 1398. Milgrom quotes from Douglas, but I cannot find the original source.

Rashi makes the following comments:

> *Zerizut* — He is alert and guards before a sin happens
> so he does not falter. And this is what it says in
> chapter *Kol ha-Basar* in tractate *Ḥullin*: "Doesn't
> *zahir* mean that he doesn't touch? No, that he is
> alert and washes his hands beforehand."
>
> *Neḳi'ut* — Clean without sin.
>
> *Perishut* — He even refrains from something permitted
> in order to be stringent on himself.
>
> *Tahor* — Clear white, and preferable [even to] *naḳi*.

Maimonides quotes the same statement with embellishment[103]:

> This is an extra measure of holiness and a path to piety:
> to be separate from people at large, to hold oneself apart
> from them, not to touch them, nor eat and drink with
> them. For setting oneself apart [*perishut*] leads to the
> purification of the body [*taharat ha-guf*] from wicked
> actions. Purifying one's body leads to sanctifying one's
> soul [*ḳedushat ha-nefesh*] from wicked character traits.
> And the holiness of the soul causes one to resemble
> the Divine Presence, as it states: "And you shall
> make yourselves holy; and you shall be holy, because
> I, God, who makes you holy, am holy" (Lev. 11:44)
> (*Tum'at Okhalin* 16:14).

Maimonides understands "separation" as physically removing
himself from the commoners, i.e., even from ordinary citizens

---

103. The *Kesef Mishnah* notes that Maimonides relies more on
the Yerushalmi version than the Bavli version.

who do not aspire to live by the highest religious standards. Then he says *taharah* means *taharat ha-guf*, "purity of the body." (This is opposed to Rashi, who reads *taharah* as freedom from sin.) Maimonides then defines *kedushah* as *kedushat ha-nefesh*, "holiness of the soul." What emerges immediately is that for Maimonides, purity is a physical and halakhic category, while holiness is a spiritual quality, applicable only to the soul; he unmistakably contrasts the physical body with the metaphysical soul.

The statement also appears in the Jerusalem Talmud, in the following order:

> Rabbi Pinhas b. Yair used to say: zeal brings cleanliness; cleanliness brings purity [*taharah*]; purity brings holiness [*kedushah*]; holiness brings humility; humility brings fear of sin; fear of sin brings piety [*hasidut*]; piety brings the holy spirit [*ruah ha-kodesh*]; the holy spirit brings resurrection of the dead; and resurrection of the dead brings Elijah the prophet, may he be remembered for good (JT *Shekalim* 9b).

The word "separation" (*perishut*) is absent. Other than that, the basic order remains intact: purity → holiness → piety. Two standard commentaries on the Jerusalem Talmud, the *Tiklin Haditin* and the *Korban ha-Edah*, provide complementary interpretations of this statement.

The *Tiklin Haditin* (Rabbi Israel of Shklov, 1770-1839) understands the passage in a concrete and physical way. He writes:

Neki'ut leads to taharah — Purity of the body when immersing requires being clean [*naki*] from any dirt [that would act as a] blockage [between him and the water] and without this he is not pure [*tahor*]. Similarly, by way of *neki'ut* of the body from any residue of sin one comes to *taharah* of the soul, which is only *tahor* when in a *naki* vessel, like a "pure and righteous soul."

Taharah leads to kedushah — Like the eating of sanctified foods [*kodshim*], foods that are treated as sanctified, or entering the sanctuary [which] requires ritual purity [*taharah*] and everyone who enters the Temple Courtyard requires immersion. Or, as it says, "They created a great fence. It once occurred that someone propositioned [a woman] for a sin. She asked him, 'Do you have 40 *se'ah* [of water to immerse in afterwards]?' He then desisted." And the Sages said, "Anywhere it says *kedushah*, that means refraining from illicit relations, as it says, 'You shall be holy'" (*Berakhot* 22a). And this is how *taharah* leads to *kedushah*.

Kedushah leads to anavah — Because he makes himself holy by the ways of *kedushah*, like the holy ones who constantly stand before God, he understands the greatness of God and the extent of His awesomeness, he becomes downtrodden and lowly in his own eyes from the fact that he cannot serve God as is proper to do before the King of Kings, the Holy One, Blessed is He. Also, [since] *kedushah* comes from avoiding women, [it is] as the Sages said, "Promiscuous ones are arrogant." And by this [avoiding promiscuity], he comes to *anavah*.

Anavah leads to fear of sin [yir'at ḥet] — Because of his humility [*anavah*] that he is disgusting and downtrodden in his own eyes he becomes afraid that someone as lowly as him should sin before the Holy and Awesome One. The lower and more downtrodden he is in his eyes, the greater the glory of Heaven is in his eyes and he knows how much sin damages all the [spiritual] worlds. And King David, because he was very humble—as it says, "and I am a worm and not a man"—said, "I will guard my ways from sinning." Similarly, if Heaven forbid one sinned in some way, he should be fearful and scared of his sin and the sin should always be before his eyes.

Fear of sin [yir'at ḥet] leads to ḥasidut — ḥasidut is the highest level of going beyond the letter of the law, as we say, "Is this not the teaching of the *ḥasadim*...?" And the Sages said, "Anyone whose fear precedes his wisdom, his wisdom will last." And they said, "An ignoramus cannot be a *ḥasid*," because via the fear of Heaven, which is a storehouse for wisdom, he comes to act beyond the letter of the law. Similarly, by fearing sin he comes to enact safeguards, as we say, tell the Nazirite to stay far away from a vineyard, which is beyond the letter of the law. And the main part of *ḥasidut* is to not be ashamed in front of people when doing things for Heaven, as it says at the beginning of *Berakhot*, "Guard my soul because I am a *ḥasid*; am I not a *ḥasid*... and I was not ashamed...." Then, when he reaches the top level of doing everything he must and

186

everything he is capable of achieving, then the rest is on God to help him and pour upon him a spirit from above, and he will merit *ruaḥ ha-ḳodesh*. It says in the Jerusalem Talmud at the end of *Sukkah* that the *simḥat bet ha-sho'evah* [water-drawing ceremony] was where they drew *ruaḥ ha-ḳodesh*, and the *ḥasidim* and men of [great] actions were there. [They drew *ruaḥ ha-ḳodesh* there] because they were joyous in their actions, and the *Shekhinah* can only rest [on someone] when there is joy, like by David, as it says, "*Then* You spoke in a vision...." This is how *ḥasidut* leads to *ruaḥ ha-ḳodesh*.

And the holy spirit [ruaḥ ha-ḳodesh] leads reviving of the dead — Because of the fact that the spirits [*ruḥot*] purify him and spirit was poured upon him from above—a spirit of *ḳedushah* and *taharah*—then it will rouse the souls [*ruḥot*] of the dead, that God will place it (these holy spirits) in them (the souls of the dead) and they will live, as it says, "And I will place My spirit in you and you will live." And the Sages said in the sixth chapter of *Pesaḥim*, "In the future, the righteous will revive the dead."

The *Ḳorban ha-Edah* takes a more conceptual approach to the statement. He writes:

Taharah — Even his earlier sins will become "white" and his soul will be purified [*tahor*].

Ḳedushah — Holiness of heart and thoughts.[104]

---

104. This is not dissimilar to how Maimonides understands *ḳedushah* in this passage.

Leads to anavah — Anyone who has a spirit of holiness [*ruaḥ ha-ḳodesh*] wants to be even holier because he will realize the scales of righteousness of other people and that his actions are not really as clear as they need be; this is the main part of *anavah*—that he understands the lack of his own value.

Leads to fear of sin [yir'at ḥet] — So that he will not say, "I can go into a marketplace of prostitutes and not sin," like King Solomon said. Since he is humble and views himself as a lowly person, he will be scared of sinning (and therefore avoid such situations).

Leads to ḥasidut — Meaning, that he will do things that are beyond the letter of the law so he does not come to do any sin.

Leads to ruaḥ ha-ḳodesh — Since he acts beyond the letter of the law, they do similarly with him from heaven— supernatural things [happen for him] and they reveal the secrets of the Torah to him.

Leads to reviving of the dead — Because he can bring *ruaḥ ha-ḳodesh* on the bones they will live, as happened with Ezekiel.

Leads to Elijah — Because before the final revival, Elijah will come.

Rabbi Pinhas b. Yair's statement has elicited many interpretations, of which we have examined four. The summary of those interpretations as related to holiness and surrounding terms is presented in the following chart.

	Rashi	Maimonides	Tiklin Ḥaditin	Korban ha-Edah
Perishut	Refrains from what is permitted, to be stringent	Setting oneself apart		
Taharah	Clear white, and preferable [even to] naki. (He defines naki as clean without sin.)	Purity of the body from wicked actions	Ritual immersion and avoidance of sexual sins	Purified from earlier sins
Kedushah	—	Sanctifying the soul from wicked character traits	Standing constantly before God and recognizing His awesomeness	Holiness of heart and thoughts
Ḥasidut	—	—	The highest level of going beyond the letter of the law	Beyond the letter of the law so he does not sin

Chapter 10

Comprehensive Theories of Holiness

Insofar as Judaism as a religion is characterized by the requirements of holiness, the problem of holiness structures the problem of religion for the Jews.

— Allen Grossman[105]

Until now, we have examined the origin of the Hebrew root *k-d-sh* and how it is in the Bible and rabbinic literature, in some cases in technical contexts and other places more broadly. This chapter will present the comprehensive theories of holiness held by classical Jewish commentaries, as well as by some non-Jewish sources that have exercised influence on traditional Jewish authorities. We will examine theories put forward by Rashi, Nahmanides, Maimonides, Judah Halevi, Gersonides, Immanuel Kant, Rabbi Samson Raphael Hirsch, Rudolf Otto, Eliezer Berkovits, and Rabbi Joseph B. Soloveitchik.

---

105. Grossman 396.

Rashi's Theory of Holiness

Rashi primarily understood holiness as preparation. According to one study, Rashi renders the word *k-d-sh* as *z-m-n*, "prepare," twelve times in his commentaries (Avinery 1949: 296). As noted above, he translates the phrase *ve-kiddashtam* (Exod. 19:10) as *ve-zimmantam she-yakhinu atzman ha-yom u-mahar*, "and prepare them that they should ready themselves today and tomorrow." In other places, he translates *k-d-sh* using the root *p-r-sh*. On Lev. 19:2, Rashi understands *kedoshim tihyu* as *hevu perushim...*, "you shall be separated from forbidden relations and from sin, for wherever you find restriction of sexual immorality, you find holiness" (on Lev. 19:2).[106] Philosophically, there is a difference between *z-m-n* and *p-r-sh*. Using *p-r-sh* is to say that the sanctification occurs at the moment of separation; while using *z-m-n* means the sanctification occurs earlier.

The nuance is easily lost, but Rashi interprets *tihyu* in this phrase as *hevu*. The word *tihyu* is a simple future, "you *will* be," while *hevu* is an imperative that means, "you *shall* be" (see *Be'er ba-Sadeh* on Rashi). However, Rashi's opinion on this matter is, to the best of my knowledge, unanimous, and everyone interprets *tihyu* as an imperative: "you *shall* be holy."[107]

---

106. *Mizrahi* points out that according to Rashi's interpretation, *kedoshim tihyu* describes the list of forbidden relations (Leviticus 18), not the list of commandments that follow it.

107. The *Baal Halakhot Gedolot* counts it as one of the 613 commandments. Maimonides believes it is an imperative (*tzivvui*) and exhortation, but does not qualify as a commandment (*mitzvah*) because it is too general (*ShM*, Principle 4). Nahmanides says it is a commandment, and in one place suggests that violationg "you shall be holy" is actionable.

Rashi also highlights the texts that describe forbidden foodstuff and forbidden worship (on Exod. 22:30 and Lev. 20:7). Harvey observes that regarding all three—forbidden relations, forbidden foods, and idolatry—Rashi uses the basic word *p-r-sh* (1977:16). Rashi adds an important component: regarding forbidden foods he writes, "If you are holy and separated [*kedoshim u-ferushim*] from the disgraces of carcasses and mauled animals, then behold you are Mine, but if not, you are not Mine" (on Exod. 22:30). He makes the same point about forbidden worship: "If you are separated from them [i.e., nations that practice idolatry], then you are Mine. But if not, then behold you belong to Nebuchadnezzar and his henchmen" (on Lev. 20:26). More broadly, he writes, "'so that you will be a holy people...' — so that you shall be holy *for Me*" (on Deut. 26:19).

Two observations can be made here. First, Rashi does not emphasize observing all of the commandments in terms of holiness; rather he only highlights forbidden relations, foods, and worship. Second, in all three cases he says that if the Jews observe these commandments then they are "to Me," i.e., they are a Godly nation. He does mention the general commandedness element at Lev. 11:45 and Deut. 14:1-2, but the recurring theme for Rashi is not the obligation, but the fulfillment, and the relationship that is generated between man and the Divine by adhering to these three sets of commandments.

Rashi certainly had his critics, first of which was Nahmanides (discussed in the next section). Rabbi S.R. Hirsch also rejects Rashi's theory, writing, "the keeping of the dietary laws merely prepares the ability" to achieve holiness, but is not itself a holy act (on Lev. 11:46-47). R. Hirsch writes in several places that the separation from the forbidden is not itself considered holiness, but it is merely a preparatory stage to achieving it.

Nahmanides' Theory of Holiness

We have already seen the development of the talmudic dictum, "sanctify yourself with what is permitted to you" (*Yevamot* 20a). Based on this passage, Nahmanides wrote:

> Someone fixated on desire would find room to be obsessed with copulating with his wife or with multiple wives, and be among those who excessively consume wine or who gluttonously devour meat, and utter profanities as he wishes, since this prohibition has not been mentioned in the Torah. Thus he will become a glutton within the confines of the Torah. Therefore, Scripture came to specify the actions that are categorically prohibited, and gave a general command that we should be separated [*p-r-sh*] from things that are permitted.[108]

David Novak explained Nahmanides' rationale as follows, "The mere observance of the legalities does not insure one of becoming a holy person, which is the ultimate purpose of the commandments" (1992: 3). R. Bahya ben Asher, of the Nahmanidean school,[109] summarizes the teaching, "If one who abstains from a forbidden food is called 'holy,' *a fortiori* one

---

108. R. Shneur Zalman of Liadi actually understood this as a biblical commandment (*Tanya* 27).
109. Nahmanides taught Rashba, who taught R. Bahya.

who abstains from permissible things is certainly worthy of being called 'holy,' for he has humbled and broken his desire in the mortar of his reason in honor of his Creator, blessed be He."[110] Furthermore, it is possible that according to Nahmanides, a violation of Lev. 19:2 was actionable by the court (see on Deut. 21:18).

The asceticism approach is also an outgrowth of a midrashic passage discussed earlier: "The Holy One, Blessed be He, said to Moses: Go say unto My children Israel, 'Just as I am separated, so you shall be separated. Just as I am holy, so you shall be holy.' This is what is written, 'You shall be holy'" (*Leviticus Rabbah* 23:4). While Rashi understands this passage as referring to the prohibited sexual acts, which are explicit in the Torah, Nahmanides understands the *perishut* of this passage to separated from even what is permitted. One of my teachers once made the remark, "Rashi says separate from the forbidden, and Nahmanides says separate from the permitted."

Nahmanides also idealizes the Nazirite as the exemplar of holiness. In asking why the Nazirite is required to bring a sin-offering upon completion of his vow, Nahmanides writes, "this man sins against his soul on the day of his completion of his Naziritehood; for until now he was separated in sanctity

---

110. Bahya 1980: 549-550. See also the position of the Hasidic Rabbi Zevi Elimelekh of Lizhensk: "Even when you are involved in what is permitted, you must be holy and separate, and not connected to corporality.... At such times, we must intend only to do His will—to proceed, using the strength derived from the eating, to the service of God and to extricate the spark of holiness, and so forth; and also in marital relations, to fulfill the commandment to perpetuate the species, but divest ourselves of any pleasure from the physical act..." (Lamm 1999: 168-169).

and the service of God, and he should therefore have remained separated forever, continuing all his life consecrated and sanctified [*nazir ve-ḳadosh*] to his God" (on Num. 6:11).[111]

However, there are some problems with Nahmanides' approach. First, there is one line of talmudic thinking that discourages additional restriction: "Are the Torah's prohibitions not enough that you come to add other prohibitions?" (JT *Nedarim* 9:1 [41b]). Similarly, it is taught elsewhere, "In the future, a person will have to give God an accounting for everything that his eyes beheld and he did not want to eat" (JT *Kiddushin* 4:12 [66b]).

Second, there is no indication in the Bible that holiness increases linearly or proportionately. In fact, the weight of evidence indicates that holiness is more like a mathematical step-function, where each level is functionally different from the one below it and above it, as seen in the Mishnah *Kelim* 1:6-9, and the congruous examples of times, persons, animals, and the material of the tabernacle fixtures (this has all been examined in earlier chapters). According to the Mishnah, the entire land of Israel has the same level of holiness, whether one step or many miles away from the walls of Jerusalem. But according to Nahmanides, holiness is like a set of mathematical *dx* integrals, increasing in infinitesimals with each withdrawal from the pleasures of the earth.

Though he does not wax large on it, Nahmanides— more than he understands holiness as abstention from the

---

111. Nahmanides' theory is intended to refute Maimonides, who asked why the Nazirite requires *kapparah,* "atonement" (Num. 6:11), and answers, "And just as the Nazirite, who separated only from wine, requires atonement, all the more so for someone who separates from everything!" (*De'ot* 3:2).

permissible—also understands holiness in terms of *devekut* (Lev. 19:3, Deut. 27:19). He defines *devekut* as either worshipping God alone, or "It is possible that the term 'cleaving' [=*devekut*] includes the obligation that you remember God and His love always, that your thought should never be separated from Him" (on Deut. 11:22). Holiness for Nahmanides has a component of asceticism and withdrawal, but just as importantly holiness is about a constant awareness of God.[112]

Maimonides' Theory of Holiness[113]

On the most basic level, Maimonides adopts the theory that holiness is synonymous with Torah-observance:

> "You shall be holy" (Lev. 19:2) and "Sanctify yourselves and be holy" (Lev. 11:44) are commandments to fulfill the entire Torah, as if it were written, "Be holy in doing all that I commanded you to do, and keep yourself from everything that I exhorted you against."… Therefore, there is no difference between saying, "You shall be holy," and saying, "Observe my commandments" (*ShM*, Principle 4).

In the *Guide*, Maimonides reiterates that holiness means observing the commandments:

> The divine words, "And you shall sanctify yourselves, and you shall be holy" (Lev. 11:44), do not refer to these

---

112. Earlier, the ideas of *imitatio Dei* and *devekut* were contrasted.
113. Though Maimonides preceded Nahmanides, the latter's theory is more unified so that has been examined first.

laws at all [how the Sabeans misunderstand holiness]. According to *Sifra*, they refer to sanctity by obedience to God's commandments. The same interpretation is given in *Sifra* of the words, "You shall be holy" (Lev. 19:2), which means obedient to His commandments. Hence the transgression of commandments is also called "uncleanness" or "defilement." This term is especially used of the chief and principal crimes, which are idolatry, adultery, and murder (*Guide* 3:47).

Maimonides introduces a wrinkle by saying that "holiness" and "uncleanness" are "especially used of the chief and principal crimes." Maimonides' choice to invoke it here, in the context of holiness and impurity, is unique. The continuation of the passage in the *Guide* identifies biblical verses that equate impurity with forbidden worship (Lev. 20:3), forbidden sexual encounters (Lev. 18:24), and murder (Num. 35:34).[114] These biblical passages use the word "defile" in a moral, rather than ritual, sense. Therefore, it seems that these three crimes are used homiletically as examples of complete transgression of the law.

Nonetheless, Maimonides identifies two specific acts that are called holy: avoidance of forbidden foods and abstention from forbidden sexual encounters:

[In the] fifth book [of the *Mishneh Torah*], I will collect the commandments of sexual transgressions and the commandments of prohibited foods, because in these

---

114. I am not aware of any verse that explicitly links holiness with not murdering

two matters God sanctified us and separated us from the other nations.... Of both of them it is said, "And I have separated you from the nations," "which I have separated you from the nations." And I have called this book *Sefer Kedushah* (*Mishneh Torah*, "Peratei ha-Sefarim").

Again, Maimonides suggests that eating and relations are proxies for the entire body of halakhic observance. Twersky notes, "Many scholars have been agitated by this grouping and have tended not to take the explanation seriously," but he then notes that there is ample evidence that this classification is "authentic" (1980: 286-287). He quotes that Philo of Alexandria "groups marriage laws and dietary laws together, for their common purpose is continence and temperance" (p. 288).

Perhaps eating and relations are almost a proxy for fulfilling the entire law. In this formulation, the law of sexual conduct is the only item to appear on both lists—the categorization of impurity or the fulfillment of holiness. To this extent, Twersky writes, "While 'holiness' is the ultimate concern and goal of all laws, there is a special nexus between holiness and the laws of this book" (p. 264).

Additionally, in two places Maimonides ostensibly takes the opinion that holiness is connected with *imitatio Dei*.

We are commanded to follow these middle paths, which are the good and just paths. As it says, "And you shall walk in His ways" (Deut. 28:9). Thus the Sages explained this commandment, "As He is called merciful, you be merciful. As He is called compassionate, you be compassionate. As He is called holy, you be holy (*De'ot* 1:6; this is a portmanteau of Lev. 19:2 and *Shabbat* 133b).

In the *Guide*, Maimonides writes similarly:

… for the chief aim of man should be to make himself, as far as possible, similar to God; that is to say, to make his acts similar to the acts of God, or as our Sages expressed it in explaining the verse, "You shall be holy" (Lev.19:2): "He is gracious, so be you also gracious: He is merciful, so be you also merciful" (*Guide* 1:54).

Maimonides also uses the Hebrew term *kedushah yeteirah*, "additional holiness." Concerning forbidden relations he writes, "… it is proper for a man to overcome his inclination in this matter and to accustom himself in an additional holiness [*kedushah yeterah*] and pure thought and a proper mindset to be protected from [violating these laws]" (*Issurei Bi'ah* 22:20). Concerning forbidden food, he writes, "Whoever is diligent in these matters brings an additional holiness and purity to his soul, and he polished his soul for the Holy One, blessed be He, as it says, 'Sanctify yourselves and you shall be holy, for I am holy'" (*Ma'akhalot Asurot* 17:32).[115] Here, even though forbidden foods and relations are already included as statutory definitions of holiness, he is introducing a supererogatory element as well.

---

115. He also uses the phrase at *Tefillin, Mezuzah, ve-Sefer Torah* 10:2, in a fundamentally different context.

In two places, Maimonides advocates holiness as a form of asceticism. In discussing the qualifications of a prophet, he writes:

> He sanctifies himself and separates from the ways of the rest of the world that walks in the darkness of the age. Rather he hastens himself and trains his soul that it should not harbor any of the transient concerns... (*Yesodei ha-Torah* 7:1).

> The Law is also intended to give its followers purity and holiness; by teaching them to suppress sensuality, to guard against it and to reduce it to a minimum (*Guide* 3:33).

One could claim that Maimonides only advocated holiness *qua* supererogation for a prophet but would not do so for a layman, but this is not decisive, especially in the passage from *Guide* 3:33. And unlike Nahmanides, he considers the Nazirite someone in need of atonement for denying himself the pleasures of the world (*De'ot* 3:2). In the case of the Nazirite, it is possible that since he prefaces his comment with the phrase *amru Ḥakhamim*, "the Sages said," he was quoting a talmudic dictum without endorsing it fully. It is also possible that on some level Maimonides agreed with his successor, Nahmanides, that holiness can indeed contain an element of superorgation and ascetism.

Maimonides has a highly complex theory about what it means to be holy, and it is comprised of several different strands:

1. There is no difference between saying "be holy" and "follow My commandments" (*ShM*, Principle 4; *Guide* 3:47). This is probably reinforced by his placement of sanctification of God's Name early in the *Mishneh Torah* (*Yesodei ha-Torah* 5:1), about which one author writes, "Maimonides… places the Sanctification of the Name as the first in his list of the practical commandments as the fundamental principle of the Torah and the basic purpose of Jewish existence" (Shapiro 1964: 70).

2. Even though holiness is observance of all the commandments, there are some whose violation is more severe (*Guide* 3:47) and observance is considered more fundamental: forbidden relations and foods, which is why he called his fifth book "the book of holiness" (*Mishneh Torah*, "Peratei ha-Sefarim").

3. In the instances of forbidden foodstuffs and forbidden relations, he uses the term "extra holiness" at the end of those two sections, to reinforce that point. While Rashi says that observing the dietary and sexual laws is an act of holiness, Maimonides embellishes that, regarding these subsets of laws, one requires "additional holiness."

4. Holiness has an aspect of *imitatio Dei* (*De'ot* 1:6; *Guide* 1:54).

5. Holiness has an ascetic tinge in some of his writings (*Yesodei ha-Torah* 7:1; *Guide* 3:33). Some of these are based on biblical sources, some on rabbinic writings, and some on philosophical teaching.

Judah Halevi (1075-1141)

Rabbi Judah Halevi explains holiness as follows:

> "Holy" expresses the notion that He is high above any attribute of created beings, although many of these are applied to him metaphorically. For this reason Isaiah heard an endless, "Holy, holy, holy" (Isa. 6:3), which meant that God is too high, too exalted, too holy, and too pure for any impurity of the people in whose midst His light dwells to touch Him. For the same reason Isaiah saw him "sitting upon a throne, high and lifted up." "Holy" is, further, a description of the spiritual, which never assumes a corporeal form, and which nothing concrete can possibly resemble. God is called the "Holy One of Israel," which is another expression for the Divine Influence connected with Israel himself and the whole of his posterity, to rule and guide them, but not to be merely in external contact with them (*Kuzari* 4:3).

The opinion of the *Kuzari* is often presented as diametrically opposed to that of Maimonides. For example, Menachem Kellner says that for Maimonides, holiness is "institutional," whereas for Halevi holiness is "instrinsic" (2003: III), but this requires some clarification. For Maimonides, holiness is primarily dependent on the commandments. A place with more commandments is holier; that is why Israel is holier than the other lands, why Jerusalem is holier than the rest of Israel, and so forth. For Maimonides, since holiness is primarily dependent on *mitzvot*, holiness is primarily a legal concept. For the *Kuzari*, holiness is not a legal concept but an objective fact, which is called "intrinsic." Kellner uses the analogy of a Geiger counter, which instead of measuring radioactivity, measures holiness. According to Kellner, this holiness-measuring device "would click every time its wand came near something holy, just as a Geiger counter clicks in the presence of radioactivity" (Kellner 2006: 43; Rynhold 2009: 108). Rynhold adds, "Thus, if I have a handful of soil from London and a handful of soil from Jerusalem, these two piles of soil really differ. The latter would have our holiness counter clicking furiously; the former would not have any activity" (109).

However, for the *Kuzari*, that holiness is not inherent as the thing-in-itself, but is still dependent on the Divine Presence (the *Shekhinah*). To this end, Halevi writes, "Whosoever prophesied did so either in the [Holy] Land, or concerning it, e.g., Abraham in order to reach it, Ezekiel and Daniel on account of it. The two latter had lived during the time of the first Temple, had seen the *Shekhinah*, through the influence of which each one who was duly prepared became of the elect, and able to prophesy" (2:14). To paraphrase *Euthyphro*, objects are holy because God chooses that status to obtain; not the other way around. Rationalists are inclined to connect the status of holiness to some operation of law, but for Halevi holiness is related to the *Shekhinah*; whether or not it generates some mandatory action, it creates the opportunity for an enhanced relationship, as in the case of prophecy. Therefore, calling this "intrinsic" holiness is imprecise. Rabbi Joseph B. Soloveitchik makes a similar point, "Nothing should be attributed *a priori* to dead matter. Objective *kedushah* smacks of fetishism" (2005b: 150).

Levi Gersonides (1288-1344)

Rabbi Levi ben Gershon, known in Hebrew as Ralbag and in English as Gersonides, was a follower of Maimonides in the deep commitment to the harmonization of Greek and Jewish thought. In his explanation of Lev. 19:2, he writes:

> "You shall be holy for I the Lord your God [am holy]" — This means you should sanctify yourselves [titkaddashu] from the deficiencies of matter [me-hisronot ha-homer] and purposefully separate as much as is possible for you, and in this way you will be similar to Him as much as possible, for I am separate from matter and clear from it in every way.

Gersonides here fuses three separate ideas in his theory of holiness. First, he accepts the notion advocated by Maimonides, but originating in Greek thought, that since matter is temporal, it is transient and flawed. Second, he accepts Nahmanides' theory that holiness means separating from the physical world; but for Gersonides, the separation is not because pleasure should be minimized, but because associating with physical matter is inherently deficient. Nahmanides and Gersonides get to the same approximate destination—that of minimizing physicality—but take different routes to arrive that that conclusion.

Third, Gersonides says that since God is free from physicality, then a person who frees himself from physicality as much as possible is in that sense emulating God. As Seymour Feldman writes, "Just as God is pure intellect, so we become truly like God, that is, incorporeal, to the extent that we follow these commandments. Holiness is for Gersonides synonymous with separation from matter and perfection of the intellect" (1997: 333).

Immanuel Kant (1724-1804)

Kant offered his own definition of holiness, one which equates holiness with the desire to to what is morally right:

> Now, *the perfect accordance of the will with the moral law is holiness*, a perfection of which no rational being of the sensible world is capable at any moment of his existence. Since, nevertheless, it is required as practically necessary, it can only be found in a progress in infinitum towards that perfect accordance, and on the principles of pure practical reason it is necessary to assume such a practical progress as the real object of our will (Greene 1929: 358, emphasis added).

There are several components here. The first is that, for Kant, holiness is an abstract concept defined as the moral law. Kant does not ascribe the attribute of holiness to individual beings (with the possible exception of what Kant calls the "Infinite Being"). Rather, holiness is an abstract concept. Roger J. Sullivan faithfully relates the above passage in clearer language:

> Holiness or moral perfection is, strictly speaking, not a possible achievement for us, and our obligation to adopt it as our supreme goal is, accordingly, a wide and

imperfect duty…. Although *the moral law commands us to be holy*, the human moral condition allows us only to progress toward holiness…. We cannot actually ever finally win the moral battle; we cannot actually achieve holiness (Sullivan 1989, emphasis added).

Kant further argued that, inherently, holiness cannot be achieved.[116] This seems paradoxical, because for Kant, the moral imperative is the greatest virtue—synonymous with holiness itself—yet it is something that can never be reached.

His argument is as follows. The moral imperative relates to duty. For Kant, a duty is something that is not to be enjoyed, but something that is done purely because of its binding and mandatory nature. If it becomes pleasurable, then he is no longer performing the act *qua* duty. Thus the act becomes "indulgent," ceases to be a duty, and fails to achieve holiness. Alternatively, if one performs these deeds and claims to understand their metaphysical nature, then he has become lost in "theosophic dreams," which is speculative and ill-grounded knowledge. Either way, the individual is condemned to ever pursue holiness yet never achieve it.

---

116. In Christian circles there was a similar debate. John Wesley, one of the co-founders of Methodism, was an English contemporary of Kant, and he believed that under the name holiness, man could achieve perfection. The Wesleyans were countered by the Keswick movement—who took their name from their convention in Keswick, England—which rejected the Wesleyan notion that man could exist in a state of sinlesseness. The Keswick movement taught that "the sinful nature is never extinguished during life on earth."

There are several points of divergence that can be highlighted. The first one, though most important, will be given the least amount of space. Trying to define one abstract term, "holiness" by means of another, "morality," is a poor language game at best, and chicanery at worst.

Second, Kant's puritanical view of duty above all may be noble, but it remains questionable. If an individual enjoys his vocation, he is still receives compensation. In fact, his employer might be pleased by the worker's enthusiasm. In a religious or moral setting, Kant is correct that there is a greater risk of engaging in ethical or religious behavior for personal gain, or purely for the sake or feeling good afterward. Nonetheless, someone who finds meaning, fulfillment—even contentment— should not be denigrated for that satisfaction, but respected. Kant and traditional Judaism clearly diverge on this point.

A third criticism of Kant is Otto's objection, "It is true that all this moral significance is contained in the word 'holy,' but it includes in addition—as even we cannot but feel—a clear overplus of meaning… if the ethical element was present at all, at any rate it was not original and never constituted the whole meaning of the word" (1958: 5). Holiness belongs squarely to the purview of religion, and to apply it elsewhere is either metaphor or poetry. Otto is correct that holiness is primarily a religious concept. This is not to deny that holiness has an ethical component, but there is a clear religious distinction between holiness and righteousness.

Whether man is able to cleanse himself of the desire to sin is a debate in Judaism. Maimonides appears to believe that such a status is possible (see *Shemonah Perakim*, ch. 6). However,

Rabbi David Zvi Hoffman points out that whenever the Hebrew word "holy" is used in regards to God, it is written *plene* קָדוֹשׁ, with the extra letter *vav*. However, when man is said to be holy, it is written without the extra *vav*, e.g., קְדֹשִׁים. Based on this observation, Rabbi Hoffman, contra Maimonides, suggests that man can only strive for perfection, but the only completely perfect being is God.

Rabbi Samson Raphael Hirsch

Rabbi Samson Raphael Hirsch equates holiness with ethics, writing that the imperative of Lev. 19:2 is "the admonition to the highest degree of moral human perfection," and "holiness, the very height of being absolutely ready for all that is good, presupposes the whole being in such a state of being penetrated by morality." Rabbi Dr. Joseph Breuer, Hirsch's grandson, similiarly understood "Israel was holy to the Lord" (Jer. 2:3) as "dedicated to God and to His moral law" (1988: 9).

Rabbi Hirsch develops a similar point regarding the *terumah* ("heave-offering"). The Hebrew word *terumah* comes from the word *le-harim*, "to lift up," which suggests that *terumah* was designated by physically lifting ("heaving") it from the pile of grain. However, Rabbi Hirsch offers a deeper understanding, "It is a 'raising' of the corporeal, the material, to holy, spiritual-moral purposes" (on Lev. 7:32).

We have already shown that holiness has a strong ethical component even from biblical times. For example, Sarna's quotation concerning the city of Nippur: "the holy city does not tolerate 'hypocrisy, distortion, abuse, malice, unseemliness, insolence, enmity, oppression, envy, force, libelous speech, arrogance, violation of an agreement, breach of contract, and abuse of a [court] verdict'" (1993: 102). Biblical sources that seem to equate this idea are Isa. 5:16, Psalms 15 and 24, and Hag. 2:12-13. Socrates also equates morality and holiness in *Euthyphro* and *Protagoras*.

Rabbi Hirsch may also have been influenced by Kant's understanding of holiness as morality.[117] It is possible that Kant's "the perfect accordance of the will with the moral law is holiness" might underlie Rabbi Hirsch's position that Lev. 19:2 is "the admonition to the highest degree of moral human perfection."[118]

Some of the criticisms of Kant can be applied to Rabbi Hirsch as well. Sol Roth writes, "While it is the case that the holy and the moral share a certain character, i.e., they both impose obligation, the two must be distinguished" (1974: 34-35). In short order, the perspective of Otto will be presented, and his critiques of Kant can be levelled against R. Hirsch as well.

Rudolf Otto (1869-1937)

Rudolf Otto was one of the first scholars in a field that would be come to be called comparative religion. He also studied Kant extensively, and wrote his dissertation on the teachings

---

117. One major difference is that for Kant an action is not ethical if it is done for the individual's benefit or pleasure, even if the action achieves the desired beneficial result. Judaism rejects this theory, and a good action done for the wrong reason is usually considered a mitzvah, e.g., "If someone says, 'I give this coin to charity so that my children will live,' or 'so that I may merit the world to come,' he is completely righteous" (*Rosh Hashanah* 4a).

118. There are other places where it seems to me that Rabbi Hirsch was influenced by Kant's philosophy.

of Martin Luther. Otto devoted his early works to the rational elements of religion; his first published work was *Naturalism and Religion*, which was released in 1907. In 1910, he voyaged around the world—including Africa, the Middle East, and the Orient—which stirred a profound interest in the mystical, non-rational, elements of religious life, which inspired Otto to author *Das Heilige* in 1917, which was translated into English in 1923, under the title *The Idea of the Holy: An Inquiry into the non-rational factor in the idea of the divine and its relation to the rational*. Although Otto is the author of eleven books, he is usually remembered for only one.

His most famous contribution is the word "numinous." Otto writes of the "numinous" that "This mental state is perfectly *sui generis* and irreducible to any other; and therefore, like every absolutely primary and elementary datum, while it admits of being discussed, it cannot be strictly defined" (1958: 7). Not dissimilarly, Abraham J. Heschel writes that holiness "is not capable of being described in terms of any other quality" (1965: 49). Otto explains that the numinous state cannot be explained—it must be experienced.

More than once, Otto addresses a purported relationship between holiness and morality. We have already seen that he wrote, "if the ethical element was present at all, at any rate it was not original and never constituted the whole meaning of the word" (1958: 5). He further dismisses holiness as ethics, writing, "once it has been grasped that *qādôsh* or *sanctus* is not originally a *moral* category at all, the most obvious rendering of the words is 'transcendent'" (52). In all of this, Otto is strongly rejecting Kant's idea that holiness is an ethical term.

Gammie identifies five categories in Otto's assessment of the non-rational:

- *tremendum*: awfulness, plenitude of power, which evokes a sense of dread and includes divine wrath.
- *maiestas*: overpoweringness, plenitude of being, absolute unapproachability.
- *energicum*: urgency, vitality, will, force, movement, excitement, activity, energy which for the mystic is experiences as "consuming fire."
- *mysterium*: being "wholly other," different, incommensurable, beyond, transcendent, supernatural.
- *fascinans*: compelling fascination, feelings of intoxication, rapturous exaltation.[119]

These are all personal responses to an encounter with the holy, although some of these sentiments are expressed in biblical verses.

To give one example, Otto focuses on the verse, "And the Lord is in His holy temple; let all the earth keep silence before Him" (Hab. 2:20). It is a sense of being overcome by God's presence, His glory, even His holiness, from which man cannot conjure a response and do naught but remain hushed overcome by this "numinous" quality. It is certainly true that the feeling of holiness can elicit these emotional responses. Otto noted that someone who has not experienced these states will have little use for his work.

Otto informs his readers that *The Idea of the Holy* is designed to address only the non-rational traditions of religious thought; the subtitle tells the reader that much. Streetman quotes from Otto himself, "I feel that no one ought to concern humself with the 'Numen ineffabile' who has not already devoted assiduous and serious study to the 'Ratio aeterna'"

---

119. The preceding five categories are taken almost verbatim from Gammie 5.

(1980: 367). Unfortunately, some readers have simultaneously ignored Otto's caveat while also taking Otto as the final word on the subject. Gammie, however, is critical of Ottos' work: "Nowhere does Otto sufficiently probe the notion that the holy calls for purity" (1989: 7).

Furthermore, Otto's categories are imprecise. These five categories are, at best, foci with indefinite boundaries sketched loosely about fixed points. There is no criterion to determine whether a specific use of "holy" should fall in one category or the other, or if each listing is mutually exclusive.

Third, Otto commits the common error of confusing holiness with other aspects of the relationship between God and man. His pages describe different types of fear, awe, terror, and dread, which sometimes correspond to the idea of holiness (see the discussion of words like *nora* above), but holiness envelops much more than just a sense of majesty and awe. Otto's work is a response to rationalists like Kant and others who drained religion from any of its mystical or metaphysical aspects, and in this effort he is praiseworthy, since religion should be considered more than merely a system of ethics. Yet in doing so, Otto appears to have wandered too far from the simple reading of the biblical text in some cases.

It is also worth pointing out Jewish responses to Otto. First, Rabbi Joseph B. Soloveitchik in one place accepts the idea of *mysterium tremendum* but relegates it to God's *middat ha-din*, attribute of justice (2008: 47-50). Here is must be stressed that Rabbi Soloveitchik did not accept the numinous and *mysterium tremendum* as the full definition of holiness (this will be discussed more fully later). Additionally, Warren

Zev Harvey adds, "The *mysterium tremendum*, the awesome consciousness of the Divine mystery, comes only after man has pushed his intellect as far as it can go" (1977: 11). Harvey, like Rabbi Soloveitchik, limits the import of the *mysterium tremendum*; Rabbi Soloveitchik did it on attributional grounds, while Harvey did it on cognitive grounds.

Despite these criticisms and limitations, Otto is important because he set out to describe the indescribable; he probably never intended to author a comprehensive view of holiness, but only to begin to put the outlines of language on some of the most ineffable human experiences. As a work of philosophy, the logical positivists would say much of it is "meaningless" (discussed later).

At the same time, many people, perhaps most, have had an ineffable religious experience at least once. I certainly have had moments of awe and dread, of overpoweringness, of chills pulsating through my frame when I am able to achive proper focus and awareness in times of prayer. Otto's work is best described as one of phenomenology or religious psychology, and when viewed in that light his work is a noble endeavor to describe some of the most complex human emotions.

Twentieth-Century Linguistics and Logical Positivism

We have seen that the Semitic root *k-d-sh* has two semantic components: "separated + elevated." These two components can be considered independently. To be considered "separated," there must be at least two sets of objects: the default set, and the separated set. If there is no act of separating, only the default set remains. If the act of separating claims everything in the default set, then the entire default set remains; there has been no act of separation.

It is more difficult to define the component "elevated." "Elevated" as a metaphor describes that God, sometimes through man's designation, favors or prefers a certain object. The object becomes "closer" (another metaphor) to Him. Hence Even-Shoshan translated k-d-sh as "elevated [na'aleh] and exalted [nisgav]."

To be holy means to enter into a unique relationship with God. This is best expressed in the verse, "Israel was holy to the Lord, the firstfruits of the harvest, whoever devoured it became guilty, evil came to them, declares the Lord" (Jer. 2:3).[120] Altschuler sees the use of the word "firstfruits" (Hebrew, reshit) as a concept of goodness, which is an argument that the "holy" is to be regarded as good or favorable from a theological perspective. Holiness would then be, in some theological sense, that which has the highest level of absolute goodness and divine favor or purpose, on account of the relationship it possesses with God.

*

Burton M. Leiser attacked Otto, using the tools of logical positivism and the premises of Jewish rationalist philosophy. Leiser says of Otto's work, "Much of this analysis is sheer nonsense, and the remainder is false" (1971: 88). His use of "nonsense" is not a term of contempt; in the positivist school, the descriptions "nonsense" and "meaningless" are used very

120. Durkheim writes, "the firstfruits of the harvest manifest the energy which they contain: here the totemic god acclaims himself in all the glory of his youth. This is why the firstfruits have always been regarded as a very sacred fruit, reserved for very holy beings" (Durkheim 1915: 379).

literally to describe a string of words that has grammatical form, but is not logically reducible to anything meaningful.

Leiser further notes that the adjective "holy" does not function like other adjectives.

> ... though the statements, "This is sandy ground" and "This is holy ground" look very much alike [from a grammatical perspective], it is evident that the adjectives are of radically different types. The word "sandy" serves not only to modify the word "ground;" it also characterizes the ground itself, describing it in such a way that anyone hearing the sentence would know just what characteristics the soil possessed.... This is clearly not the case with the word "holy" (p. 90).

The way in which an adjective relates to the noun is a problem for philosophers of language, and as Leiser notes, it is a more challenging problem for adjectives of metaphysics. Leiser responds to this problem by saying that "holy" is a "convenient shorthand expression for a series of relationships that persons bear to one another with respect to that thing, and, possibly, to the thing itself."[121] He concedes that the phrase "holy ground" does not possessing *meaning* in the strict sense; the determining factor is the "series of relationships" that are present.

---

121. Leiser 1971: 90. Durkheim explains "respect" as follows: "We say that an object, whether individual or collective, inspires respect when the representation expressing it in the mind is gifted with such a force that it automatically causes or inhibits actions, *without regard for any consideration relative to their useful or injurious effects*" (Durkheim 1915: 237, emphasis original). In other words, "respect," like the holy, is categorical.

Since Leiser is writing from a rabbinic perspective, that "series of relationships" is biblical and rabbinic legislation, "laws which we would today class as a conglomeration of ritual, cultic regulations and ethical norms, but which the Jews of ancient Israel and the Pharisees treated as being equal in their power to make of Israel a holy nation" (p. 91).

The philosopher William P. Alston argued that the standards of meaningfulness needed to be relaxed, since the positivists' requirements sometimes made it impossible to define even basic, ordinary, and concrete nouns. For example, he writes, "In primitive religion, ritual acts may focus around a bull, a mountain, or a sacred fire, without there being an explicit account of what gives these objects the significance they are felt to have" (1964: 59). Here it contrasts linguistic weight ("explicit account") with the experiential value ("the significance they are felt to have"). The ritual acts that Alston describes have meaning for the person experiencing them, even though the participant may be incapable of describing the experience. (The similarity to Otto here should be apparent.)

But though Alston advocated looser criteria for meaning, he still required some standard of meaningfulness. Alston concedes that some "sources are reporting a distinct sense of something's (taken by them to be God) *presenting* itself to their awareness in generically the same way that as that in which physical objects present themselves to our awareness in sense perception" (p. 16). In other words, for the one who has the experience, there is no cognitive difference between experiencing a being contained within four walls of a room, or experiencing a divine, ineffable, flash of holiness. Nonetheless, he writes, "I doubt very much that any consistent account of religious experience can be found in the works of any of these people" (p. 16, n. 5).

In the earlier lexical analyses it has been argued that the word k-d-sh, "holy," frequently aligns with words for "separation" as well as words for "elevation." Both components (separation + elevation) are essential for understanding holiness. Otto, for example, by focusing on a narrow experience of holy, overlooks the idea of "separation" embedded in holiness. Judaism does not accept holiness merely as an emotion or feeling without an actional component.

At the same time, horizontal separation is not equivalent to separation by elevation. As Nahmanides stresses, someone so inclined can find a way to adhere punctiliously to every detail of the Torah and still be characterized as a *naval*—a boor, glutton, and knave. We might not be able to point to a specific statute that this glutton is violating, but we would not view him as an exemplar worthy of admiration and emulation. Such an individual might have separated himself from the expressly forbidden, but we would not say that he is of an elevated and refined character. Therefore, it is important, not just linguistically but theologically as well, to emphasize the two components.

Eliezer Berkovits

In 1969, Eliezer Berkovits, one of the more controversial Jewish philosophers of the twentieth century, wrote an essay entitled "The Concept of Holiness." His essay addresses and rejects three separate theories. (In the following presentation, I have

217

reordered his arrangement, but sought to be faithful to his ideas. The ordinal numbering that appears below is my arrangement of Berkovits's thoughts.)

First, he quotes a series of nineteenth-century authors who maintain that "holy" is a placeholder term for God or Godlike. He quotes from A.B. Davidson that "'holy' does not express any definite attribute of the deity. It is a rather general notion of what is meant by the godhead."[122] He quotes similar ideas from W. Robertson Smith and H. Wheeler Robinson. But this mode of interpretation is not isolated to nineteenth-century scholars. Allen Grossman writes, "Holiness is the word by which men describe God... because it is the word by which God describes himself," where he invokes, "You shall be holy, for I, the Lord your God, am holy" (Lev. 19:2).[123] Shalom Paul similarly writes that holiness is "the attribute of his very own being" (1991: 129). Berkovits disagrees with this analysis and argues that to use "holy" as a proxy word for God is too vague to be useful, either exegetically or theologically.[124]

122. Berkovits 2002: 309. Lasine also quotes from Olyan that holiness is God's "quintessential characteristic" (Lasine 2010: 50).
123. Grossman 389.
124. Well before Berkovits, one key talmudic passage makes it clear that holiness is not synonymous with Godliness: "Rabbi Yohanan said, 'Wherever you find [mention] of the strength of the Holy One, Blessed is He, you find [mention] of His humility... 'For thus says the high and lofty one who inhabits eternity, whose name is Holy,' and it is written afterward, '[I am] with those who are contrite and humble in spirit' (*Megillah* 31a, quoting Isa. 57:15). In Rabbi Yohanan's analysis, God's might is represented by the words 'high,' 'lofty,' and 'holy,' while God's humility is represented by His being "near those who are contrite and humble in spirit." For our purposes, these two attributes are not synonymous and therefore God and His Holiness cannot be one and the same.

Second, he addresses the theory that holiness is related to ethics. In his essay, he does not mention Kant explicitly, but he almost certainly had the Prussian in mind when considering this theory. Berkovits writes, "Holiness is not, for example, ethics. Holiness is a specifically religious category. The highest form of ethics may be unrelated to holiness. It is a noble thing to do the good for its own sake, but it is not holiness" (2002: 284). Berkovits's criticism of Kant echoes Otto's critique, quoted earlier, "It is true that all this moral significance is contained in the word 'holy,' but it includes in addition—as even we cannot but feel—a clear overplus of meaning... if the ethical element was present at all, at any rate it was not original and never constituted the whole meaning of the word" (Otto 1958: 5).

Third, Berkovits shifts his attention to Otto's theories. Berkovits acknowledges the existence of the *mysterium tremendum*, but writes, "God relates himself to the world as the source of human salvation, as the one who is near, notwithstanding his being Wholly Other" (2002: 300). One of the common criticisms of Otto is that his work focuses largely on themes of fear, awe, and mystery, which can be appropriate reactions to the presence of God, but these themes are not necessarily associated with holiness. Berkovits goes further, saying that the *mysterium tremendum* is dangerously close to a theory of an "almost demonic divine mightiness which spells danger for everyone who comes near it" (301). In response, he emphasizes that, "It is not the approach that is dangerous, but the wrong approach."

Berkovits settles on a theory that holiness is synonymous with divine closeness, writing, "Far from signifying separateness, the idea of the holy conveys a sense of intimacy and relatedness."[125] He starts his study with an examination of the verse, "Holy, holy, holy is the Lord of hosts; the whole world is filled with His glory" (Isa. 6:3).[126] Berkovits says "holy, holy, holy" represents God's immanence (nearness), and "Lord of hosts" represents his transcendence (beyondness). He contrasts two divine sobriquets, *Tzeva'ot*, "Lord of hosts," and *Kedosh Yisra'el*, "Holy One of Israel." He suggests that the divine name "Holy One of Israel" is primarily associated with joy and protection, whereas "Lord of hosts" is typically associated with themes of destruction and retribution. He draws further support from the verse, "I shall not execute My fierce wrath to destroy Ephraim, because I am God, and not a man, the Holy One in your midst, and I will not enter the city" (Hos. 11:9).[127] When God is understood as the Holy One of Israel, says Berkovits, it is in His capacity as protector and defender. He writes, "the Holy One is 'in your midst.' His signs are neither fury nor anger, but compassion and love" (252).

---

125. Berkovits 2002: 252. Milgrom makes a similar comparison on semantic, not philosophical grounds, comparing *k-r-b* to *k-d-sh* (2001: 2381). See also Isa. 63:11.

126. The Hasidic movement views the verse as two contrasting halves: "Holy, holy, holy is the Lord of hosts," which contrasts with "the whole world is filled with His glory." The first half teaches that God is distant and cannot be known, not dissimilar to Otto's *mysterium tremendum*. The second half teaches God's closeness, and Dr. Lamm writes that this "is the locus classicus for the hasidic doctrine of divine immanence" (1999: 21 n. 44).

127. The meaning of the word *be'ir* in this verse is very unclear. It might mean *be-ir*, "in a [the] city," or it might come from the root *b-'-r*, "burning, furious."

Berkovits then focuses on the verse, "And the Lord of hosts is uplifted in justice, the holy God is sanctified in *tzedakah*" (Isa. 5:16) (p. 255). Berkovits takes the words as contrasts, "*Mishpat* is justice based on adherence to the law; *tzedaka* is doing right with charity and compassion" (255). He also quotes from two other verses that relate holiness with divine closeness:

- And Moses said to Aaron: This is what the Lord spoke, saying: By those close [*k-r-b*] to me I will be sanctified [*k-d-sh*], and in front of the entire people I will be honored; and Aaron was silent (Lev. 10:3).
- And [Moses] spoke to Korah and to his entire assembly, saying: In the morning the Lord will make known who is His and who is holy [*k-d-sh*], and He shall make him draw near [*k-r-b*] to Him, and whoever He chooses shall draw near [*k-r-b*] to Him (Num. 16:5).

Berkovits explains the second verse, writing, "Holiness, nearness, and being chosen are mentioned and related to each other," and "to sanctify means 'to choose in order to bring near'" (280). Propp also hints at, but not does fully endorse, this theory (2006: 430).

Despite the attractiveness of this theory, two of his prooftexts, Lev. 10:3 and Num. 16:5, do not indicate nearness, but divine wrath. The first verse culminates the narrative of Nadab and Abihu, the two sons of Aaron who perished for bringing an alien fire before God. The second verse is the fulcrum of the rebellion of Korah, who was eventually swallowed by the ground beneath him.

An additional difficulty for Berkovits is the repeated use of the phrase, "any stranger that approaches [k-r-b] shall be put to death" (Num. 17:28).[128] Thus any theory of holiness as divine compassion and nearness probably needs further refinement. Man is permitted to draw near to God, but as Berkovits notes, "It is not the approach that is dangerous, but the wrong approach" (301). There are places that k-r-b is used as a positive, desirable quality, such as "the nearness [k-r-b] of God is good for me" (Ps. 73:28, cf. Ps. 103:1), but these verses do not equate holiness with divine closeness.

However, the liturgy is more favorable to Berkovits's theory. For example, the festival *Amidah* includes the words, "You have chosen [b-ḥ-r] us from all the nations… and sanctified [k-d-sh] us with Your commandments, and brought us close [k-r-b], our King, to Your service." Here, k-d-sh, "sanctify," and k-r-b, "bring close," are used in poetic parallelism.

In summary, Berkovits systematically rejects three of the common theories—(1) holiness as a synonym for Godliness, (2) holiness as a mere ethical construct, and (3) holiness as *mysterium tremendum*—in favor of the theory that holiness is divine immanence, closeness, and compassion. His conclusion, though incompatible with the biblical verses, is amply present in rabbinic writings, especially in liturgical texts.

We can present a spectrum of opinions of holiness as follows. On one extreme sits Kant, who has removed holiness from any religious meaning at all, and equated it with ethical behavior. The other extreme, the mystical experience, is that holiness is

---

128. See Milgrom 1970: 206, esp. n. 20, where he says that in Bibilical Hebrew, k-r-b does not mean "draw near" in a neutral sense, but "encroach."

entirely numinous and non-rational (Otto). Berkovits rejects both Kant and Otto, instead claiming that holiness is divine immanence and compassion. Holiness is a guiding religious principle, and as such, it contains (and probably always has contained) an ethical component. But the equation of holiness with ethics is mistaken. The other side is also misleading. Holiness is not an endless pursuit of ephemeral emotional highs at the expense of all else; it is part of a framework that also involves adherence to law, both ritual and civic, within a religious framework.

Rabbi Joseph B. Soloveitchik's Theory of Holiness

Rabbi Soloveitchik's theory of holiness will be considered through his work *Halakhic Man* (1983), in which he creates a dichotomy (a Hegelian dialectic), pitting two archetypes, two Platonic ideals, against each other: cognitive man and *homo religiosus*. Cognitive man seeks to understand; he cannot tolerate mystery or obfuscation, but he is apathetic to ruminations of the transcendent and unconcerned with the otherworldly. *Homo religiosus* is fascinated by the mystery of the cosmos; he seeks out heaven and feels confined in the shackles of time-and-space existence. In true Hegelian fashion, Rabbi Soloveitchik's resolution is the *ish ha-halakhah*, the "man of Jewish law," i.e., the halakhic man.

For Rabbi Soloveitchik, the *mysterium tremendum* belongs to the realm of the *homo religiosus*, who "is intrigued by the mystery of existence—the *mysterium tremendum*—and wants to emphasize that mystery: "He gazes at that which is obscure without the intent of explaining it" (7). Elsewhere Rabbi

Soloveitchik understands *mysterium tremendum* as part of the Divine attribute of justice (2008: 50), rather than the attribute of mercy. In other words, Rabbi Soloveitchik only accepts Otto's *mysterium tremundum* with qualification.

For Rabbi Soloveitchik, Judaism does not prize the *homo religiosus* but the halakhic man:

> Halakhah aims to sanctify man's body, refine the bestial aspects of human life with all their lusts and drives, and raise them to the level of divine service. But this refining process does not take place in a crucible of denial and deprivation; [it occurs by] stamping the natural aspects of human existence with direction and purposefulness. Combining the beast in man with his divine image purifies and sanctifies the body. This union is accomplished by imposing the yoke of the halakhic commandments on the body (2008: 111).[129]

Earlier we saw that according to Nahmanides, the Nazirite was holy because "he was separated in sanctity and the service of God, and he should therefore have remained separated forever, continuing all his life consecrated and sanctified to his God." However, Rabbi Soloveitck rejects that theory: "The telos of Naziritehood is to sanctify bodily existence, not to avoid it. On

---

129. Similarly, "Halakhic Judaism sanctifies the profane, purifies it of the pollution it has absorbed..." (p. 133). In some places Rabbi Soloveitchik connects the idea of holiness with *imitatio Dei*, and I will not be bold enough to say he did not mean to assert such a relationship, but he spends much more time developing the idea of holiness as sanctifying the earthly.

the contrary, the Nazirite is forbidden to become ritually impure through contact with the dead" (2008: 114). The Nazirite, whom Nahmanides considered the paradigm of withdrawal, is lauded by Rabbi Soloveitchik not for his withdrawal but for his sanctification of *bodily* existence.

Rabbi Soloveitchik repeatedly makes the point that holiness is earthly, not otherwordly, when viewed through the lens of *halakhah*: "It is not anything transcendent that creates holiness but rather the visible reality—the regular cycle of the natural order" (1983: 20-21); "Holiness means the holiness of earthly, here-and-now life" (33); "Halakhic man craves to bring down the divine presence and holiness into the midst of space and time, into the midst of finite, earthly existence" (41).

Otto developed the idea of createdness and creaturehood, the grandeur and lowliness of the individual, but he does not develop any notion of commandedness. Man in his greatness (as a being created by God), or his worthlessness (a low being compared with the Infinite), experiences the holy as the numinous. However, man as a *commanded being* experiences the holy not through the numinous, not through a *mysterium*, but through *halakhah*, the dictates of Jewish law that were given by God with this express purpose. Even today, man might experience the numinous, but it is just a feeling unless it is manifest in some halakhic act.

Judaism is not predicated on superstition; it is a religion built on commandments from the Almighty. A superstitious person believes that objects, utterances, places, or actions have some sort of inherent potency, while in religion, value is solely ascribed by God:

Kedushah, under a halakhic aspect, is man-made; more accurately, it is a historical category. A soil is sanctified by historical deeds performed by sacred people, never by any primordial superiority. The halakhic term *kedushat ha-aretz*, the sanctity of the land, denotes the consequence of a human act, either conquest (heroic deeds) or the mere presence of the people in that land (intimacy of man and nature). *Kedushah* is identical with man's association with Mother Earth. Nothing should be attributed a priori to dead matter. Objective *kedushah* smacks of fetishism (2005b: 150).

For Rabbi Soloveitchik, holiness is not a standalone category but a relational one. Neither is holiness merely divine closeness, as Eliezer Berkovits argued using the root *ḳ-r-b*; as discussed earlier, approaching God the wrong way is dangerous. The safe approach to God is the *halakhah*, literally, "the way." The *Shekhinah* (Divine Presence) chooses to repose in certain places, when pursued with the proper care, where man can find access to God:

The concept of holiness is rooted in the attachment between man and God within the framework of real life. According to the Halakhah, the holiness of certain places and times is identical with the influence of the *Shekhinah* in the here-and-now. The Land of Israel is holy because the *Shekhinah* and prophecy are found there (2008: 84).

Thematic Arrangement of the Theories of Holiness

It is also be constructive to rearrange these sources thematically, in which case five approaches emerge, which we can call (1) congruity, (2) contextuality, (3) supererogation, (4) *imitatio Dei*, (5) ethics.

Congruity

This opinion says that holiness is congruous with observing the entire Torah. As mentioned earlier, there are no less than four verses that explicitly equate holiness with observing the entire Torah (Exod. 19:5-6, Num. 15:40, Deut. 26:17-19, Deut. 28:9), and potentially three other verses (Lev. 19:2, Lev. 20:7, Deut. 33:3-4). This idea is also present in the Talmud (*Shabbat* 55a), *Sifra*,[130] Maimonides, (*ShM*, Principle 4, *Guide* 3:47), and Ibn Ezra on Deut. 28:9. This is also in the standard formula of benediction, *asher ḳiddeshanu be-mitzvotav*, "who has sanctified us with his commandments."[131]

---

130. Other midrashim connect the commandments with purity, e.g., "Rav said: The commandments were only given for the purpose of purifying [*tz-r-p*] the world" (*Genesis Rabbah* 44:1, *Leviticus Rabbah* 13:3). Nahmanides comments, "that they [the Jews] might become like 'refined silver, for he who refines silver does not act without purpose, but to remove therefrom any impurity" (on Deut. 22:6).

131. This congruity approach might also explain the Midrash, "R. Hiyya taught that this section was said in front of the entire congregation because the majority of Torah principles are dependent on it. R. Levi said it is because the Decalogue is contained therein" (*Leviticus Rabbah* 24:5).

Contextuality

This opinion says we should look at the context in which holiness is mentioned, specifically which subsets of commandments are referred to by the term "holy." Those include the dietary laws (Exod. 22:30), the prohibition of idolatry (Deut. 7:5-6, 14:1-2), and the laws of sexual relations (Rashi on Lev. 19:2). Maimonides includes the dietary and sexual laws in his *Sefer Ḳedushah*, and Philo of Alexandria made the same identification.

Supererogation

According to this opinion, holiness is supererogation, asceticism, and abstaining even from what is permitted, lest one be a glutton but not violate any technical commandment. This opinion has seeds in the Talmud but is championed more famously by Nahmanides. It is also present in Maimonides in passing (e.g., *Yesodei ha-Torah* 7:1).

Imitatio Dei

This interpretation says that being holy is imitating God, who is holy. This is the opinion of Philo of Alexandria (*Decalogue* 100), Abba Shaul (*Shabbat* 133b), and one passage in Maimonides (*De'ot* 1:6).

Ethics

This opinion might have roots in Isaiah's phrase *niḳdash bi-tzedaḳah*, and is championed most famously by Rabbi Samson Raphael Hirsch, who writes that holiness is "the admonition to the highest degree of moral human perfection."

Conclusion

This work has attempted to analyze the word "holy" from historical, exegetical, and philosophical perspectives.

Historical Perspectives

I have attempted to demonstrate that the root *ḳ-d-sh* experienced a development in meaning. In pre-biblical times, it could refer to something almost capricious. The Bible, in response to this, understands holiness primarily as mitzvah-observance. The rational element is much more present in Scripture than in neighboring texts. This is one of the most dramatic ways in which the Bible forcefully repudiated its surrounding culture. The current evidence indicates that in the ancient Near East, holiness could only be ascribed to deities and royalty, never to the laity. If this is indeed true, then the Bible introduced a great innovation in stipulating that the laity was able to achieve holiness in ways previously unknown.

Furthermore, the Bible does not contain any explicit reference to the idea of abstention or supererogation in the name of holiness. I have argued that these ideas were introduced in post-exilic Judaism. There are several key talmudic passages that highlight this idea of abstention, while there are no parallel biblical passages that explicitly advocate for asceticism.

We have also observed, from a historical perspective, that the Medieval and modern authorities have offered their own interpretations. In the Middle Ages, when many authorities attempted reconciliation between the Bible and Greek thought, holiness became associated with withdrawal from physical matter, since the Greeks had a negative attitude about physicality. We have also shown how different Jewish authorities accepted Greek theories in some cases and roundly rejected them in other cases. And certain authorities, like the *Kuzari*, never felt beholden to Greek thought in the first place.

Several centuries later, in the age of Kant, there was a rejection of mysticism, so holiness was reinterpreted primarily in its ethical component. Rabbi Samson Raphael Hirsch and Hermann Cohen emphasized the ethical component in holiness. Then a response, associated closely with Otto, occurred when holiness was again reanalyzed in its non-rational aspect. I have attempted to show that Rabbi Soloveitchik synthesized the work of much of his predecessors, accepted the *mysterium tremendum* in terms of the *middat ha-din*, but adamantly argued that holiness is a halakhic term, not a mystical one.

Exegetical Perspectives

The root *k-d-sh* appears about 900 times in the Hebrew Bible. While it may be impossible to find a definition to satisfy every usage, I have tried to map how the word is applied in Tanakh. There is none as holy as God, but the word "holy" can apply to other objects as well. When people are said to be holy, it means in terms of following the commandments. Some verses refer to holiness as keeping the commandments *in toto* (e.g., Exod. 19:5-6). Other verses single out certain sets of commandments under the rubric of holiness—the dietary laws, absention from idolatry, and proper sexual conduct. I have attempted to show how this is the simple meaning—the *peshat*—in verses where people are described as holy.

I found it extremely useful and informative to analyze how the Tanakh uses the term holy: in what contexts, in describing what behaviors, and with what frequency. This point is of utmost importance because we have said that holiness appears in many contexts, and it is an inherently plastic term. Therefore, before we can transition to philosophical argumentation, we must be cognizant of how the Bible itself uses the term. Prior chapters contains charts, tallies, and rosters of how the term is used, and it is unmistakable that holiness is directly tied with mitzvah-observance.

To take it one step further, we may say that when God is spoken of as "holy," that is in an absolute sense. God's holiness is unique and incomparable. (However, we have also shown that God and His Holiness are not synonyms, based on Rabbi Yohanan's opinion in the Talmud.)

When "holy" is used of God, it is in an absolute sense, and when "holy" is used of anything else, it is in a relational sense.

Philosophical Perspectives

The root *k-d-sh* does not primarily mean "separated." It is true that the root *k-d-sh* contains the semantic component "separated," but that is just a part of the meaning, not the entire meaning. The root *k-d-sh* means "separated + elevated." The word means both things at once; venturing too far in one direction drains the word of any religious meaning, and venturing too far in the other direction abandons the obligation to make distinctions, an act obligatory to religious life.

While Rashi's comments on *k-d-sh* sometimes include the root *p-r-sh*, "separated," I do not believe he meant to give a lexicographical pronouncement that *kedushah* is synonymous with *perishut*. Rather, Rashi was highlighting that one semantic component of "holiness" is "separation." As has been discussed, in other places Rashi highlights the semantic component of "elevation," specifically with the word *li*, "to Me" (e.g. on Lev. 20:26 and Deut. 26:19).

The Component "Separated"

If we accept that "holy" has the component "separated," then it must be asked: separated from what? At the simplest level, according to Rashi and at least one opinion of Maimonides, "holy" means separated from that which is forbidden. Rashi also adds a wrinkle that it means *separated* from the surrounding heathen nations. This answer appears to be the most reliant on the biblical verses.

Others like Nahmanides and Gersonides theorize that "separated" means separated from physicality. (This theory is also present in some Maimonidean passages.) According to this interpretation of "separated," holiness is a withdrawal from physicality. I have attempted to show that this theory is based on a fusion of biblical and Greek thought. Such fusion does not delegitimize the theory; rather it shows the rigor of the Jewish tradition in using biblical texts to achieve a synthesis of Jewish tradition and philosophical rigor.

Thus there are no less than three meanings of the component "separated": separated from what is forbidden, separated from the heathen nations, and separated from physical, corruptible matter.

The Component "Elevated"

We can say the holy is "elevated" in at least two ways. First, we can say the elevation comes about by scrupulous adherence to the commandments. This is the theory of the rationalists like Maimonides. Alternatively, "holy" could mean "elevated" by means of entering into an enhanced and special relationship with God.

For Maimonides, the land of Israel is holy because there are certain commandments that apply nowhere else but the holy land. For the *Kuzari*, Israel is a place of greater Divine Presence. The former is objective, measurable, and carries immediate legal ramification; it also fits more smoothly with the strictures of analytic philosophy. The latter approach is far less measurable and less favored by the rationalists, but opens the worshipper to a much deeper relationship with God. Both lines of thinking are prevalent throughout the vast corpus of rabbinic literature.

"Holy" as God's Essence or an Attribute

We have also analyzed sources about whether "holiness" is a synonym for "Godliness" or not. To put this in philosophical, rather than literary, terms: some sources state that "holiness" represents the essence of God; other sources suggest that "holiness" is one of God's attributes but is not a term of His essence. We have seen that holiness *qua* essence might be present at, "To whom shall you compare Me and who shall I be compared to, says Kadosh" (Isa. 40:25). Shalom Paul states that holiness is "the attribute of [God's] very own being." It appears to me that academics, Jewish or not, are more inclined to take the approach that holiness is a term of God's essence.

However, Rabbi Yohanan contrasts God's holiness and God's humility (*Megillah* 31a), which suggests that holiness is one attribute of God but does not represent His essence. This approach may also be implied by Maimonides: "As He is called compassionate, you be compassionate. As He is called holy, you be holy" (*De'ot* 1:6). Eliezer Berkovits also rejected the idea that "holy" is merely a placeholder term for "Godlike." While there is an argument to be made for both sides, I prefer the argument that "holy" is an attribute of God, not a term of His essence.

Different Interpretive Traditions

I began researching this topic at a time when I was entrenched in analytic philosophy. As such, I was convinced that for "holiness" to mean anything at all, it had to be reducible to something more objective. And I quickly found that Rashi, Maimonides, and many biblical and talmudic sources showed that holiness is reducible to following the commandments, either *in toto* or in specific subsets—proper conduct in diet, intimacy, and worship. Then again, I discovered many people who disagreed, such as the *Kuzari* and Nahmanides; they say that holiness represents entering into a relationship with God (e.g., *devekut*), and they do not view holiness merely through the lens of halakhic strictures.

All of these are traditional understandings of holiness; I have tried to present them as fairly and accurately as possible, making the strongest case for each theory, but also pointing out where later authorities have observed weaknesses. I have also tried to operate with the assumption that for every criticism that Nahmanides, for example, might put forth against Rashi, Rashi would have had an answer had he been able to respond. Numerous disputes have existed between these classical commentaries, and it is not necessarily incumbent to draw a conclusion about which one is right, provided each side offer sound support, and we are patient enough to listen.

Obligation and Fulfillment

Holiness is a both an obligation and a fulfillment. Its obligation stems from numerous biblical sources commanding us to be holy. Whether one understands holiness as observance, or entering into a relationship with the Divine, there is a clear commandment explicit in these verses. Should one fail to realize that potential and squander the exhortation to holiness, a certain baseline holiness nonetheless remains. That is the holiness of obligation.

However, we are commanded to move holiness from the theoretical to the practical, from the potential to the kinetic. Whether holiness means separating from a subset of the laws (Rashi), adherence to all of the commandments (Maimonides), or a life of asceticism (Nahmanides), that call is there, always present and ready to be fulfilled. A person might have inherent holiness regardless of his behavior, but that is the holiness of obligation. The holiness of fulfilment is even greater.

Human existence, in all aspects of life, hinges on how one's free will is exercised. God has presented mankind the obligation, the mandate, and the divine imperative to obey the religious doctrine; this is the holiness of obligation. The holiness of fulfullment is whether man, in exercising his freedom of the will, decides whether to ignore this obligation or to embrace it and fulfill that Divine calling.

Primary Source Index

7:6,   75 n., 132,
        134-136,
        143
8:10,   86
11:22, 196
14:1-2, 134-136,
        192, 228
14:1,   133
14:4-5, 120
14:21, 133
15:7-11,156
15:9,   33, 75, 129,
        131
20:5,   35
22:6,   227 n.
22:9,   27, 29 n.,
        31
23:10, 140
23:15, 29 n., 139-
        140, 143
23:17, 31
23:18, 29 n.
26:15, 61
26:17-19, 136-137,
        227
26:18-19, 133
26:19, 75 n., 192
27:19, 196
28:9,   133, 136-
        137, 144,
        175, 177,
        198, 227
32:51, 71-72, 80,
        83
33:3-4, 133, 136-
        137
33:3,   86

Joshua
5:15,   95, 104
6,   99
6:18-19,70

6:19,   75 n.
6:24-26,120
7,   29 n.
7:1,   71
20:2,   33
20:7,   33
24:19, 145

Judges
13,   69
17:3,   75 n.

1 Samuel
1:9,   139 n.
1:11,   86
1:19,   141
2:2,   30
6:19,   151
7:1,   44 n., 151
21:4-7, 29 n.
21:5,   46
28:6,   29 n.

2 Samuel
6:6-7, 151
8:11,   75 n.
11:4,   26, 40, 75 n.

1 Kings
8:63-64,34
9:7,   75 n.
18:28, 135

2 Kings
4:9,   90
10:20, 75 n.

Isaiah
1:4,   68, 147
4:3,   156 n.
5:16,   81, 144,
        146-147,
        209, 221

6:3,   59, 146-
        148, 202,
        220
6:5-7, 40 n.
6:5,   74
8:13,   152
10:17, 28, 153
29:13, 151
29:23, 84, 131,
        152
40:25, 77, 147,
        176
43:15, 117 n.
47:11, 40 n.
52:1,   105
57:15, 63, 78, 218
        n.
62:12, 71
66:7,   157

Jeremiah
1:5,   29 n., 33,
        131
2:3,   75 n., 208,
        214
2:22,   40 n.
4:14,   40 n.
6:4,   29 n.
6:10,   73
22:7-9, 152
31:22, 61, 144,
        147
51:27-28, 29 n.
51:28, 152
52:1,   74

Ezekiel
11:16, 110
16:9,   42
23:38, 46, 118
28:14, 28
28:22, 59, 81

ROOTS INDEX

A Note About Transliteration

In an effort to make the subject matter as accessible as possible, I have minimized the amount of academic transliterations. For example, both *tet* and *tav* are transliterated *t*. I have also transliterated ה as *h*, which is becoming more familiar. I have also found transliterating ו is more accessible with a *v* rather than *w*.

For ק, I have settled on *k*, since *k* is too interchangeable with כ, and *q* is jarring to many readers; especially since the Hebrew word for "holy" contains the letter ק, I felt it proper to differentiate in this case by use of *k*.

In rare cases I have used academic transliteration of vowels, but only when I thought their omission would be more confusing than their inclusion.

For Semitic languages other than Hebrew, I have preserved the academic style. And I have been faithful in direct quotations to the original; some sources are more academic and some are more popular. This means ק variously appears as *k*, *ḳ* and *q* throughout the book, ט appears as both *t* and *ṭ*, and ש as both *sh* and *š*.

Hebrew roots are written with a dash between the letters for convenience, e.g., *ḳ-d-sh*, not *kdsh*. However, for longer Semitic inscriptions I have not included such dashes.

Abbreviations Used

ANET. James Pritchard. *Ancient Near Eastern Texts Relating to the Study of the Old Testament.* Princeton: Princeton University Press, 1950.

BDB. The Brown-Driver-Briggs Hebrew and English Lexicon. Peabody, Mass.: Hendrickson, 1997.

BWL. Babylonian Wisdom Literature. Ed. W.G. Lambert. Oxford: Clarendon, 1960.

CAD. The Assyrian Dictionary of the Oriental Institute of the University of Chicago (CAD). Chicago: Oriental Institute, 1956-.

DCH. The Dictionary of Classical Hebrew. Ed. David J.A. Clines Sheffield: Sheffield Academic Press, 1993-2011.

DNWSI. Dictionary of the North-West Semitic Inscriptions. Eds. Hoftijzer and Jongeling. 2 vol. Brill, 1997.

HALOT. The Hebrew & Aramaic Lexicon of the Old Testament. Eds. Ludwig Koehler and Walter Baumgartner. New York: Brill, 1994-2000.

KAI. Kanaanäishe und aramäische Inschriften I-III. Eds. H. Donner and W. Röllig.

KJV. King James Version. Originally published 1611.

NETS. *A New English Translation of the Septuagint.* Oxford: Oxford University Press, 2009.

NRSV. New Revised Standard Version. Originally published 1989.

OED. The Compact Edition of the Oxford English Dictionary: Complete Text Reproduced Micrographically. 2 vols. Oxford: Oxford University Press, 1971.

PhM. Maimonides' *Perush ha-Mishnayot* ("Commentary on the Mishnah"). Twelfth Century.

ShM. Maimonides' *Sefer ha-Mitzvot* ("Book of Commandments"). Twelfth century.

TDOT. Theological Dictionary of the Old Testament. Eds. G. Johannes Botterweck, Helmer Ringgren, Heinz-Josef Fabry. 15 vols. Grand Rapids, MI: Eerdmans, 1974-2006.

Bibliography

Alcalay 1962: Alcalay, Reuben. *The Complete English-Hebrew Dictionary*. Hartford: Prayer Book Press, 1962.

Alston 1964: Alston, William P. *Philosophy of Language*. Englewood Cliffs, N.J.: Prentice-Hall, 1964.

Alston 1991: Alston, William P. *Perceiving God: The Epistemology of Religious Experience*. Ithaca: Cornell University Press, 1991.

Angel 2013: *Through an Opaque Lens: The Bible Refracted Though Eternal Rabbinic Wisdom*. Revised Second Edition. New York: Kodesh Press, 2013.

Aster 2012: Aster, Shawn Zelig. *The Unbeatable Light*. Munster: Ugarit-Verlag, 2012.

Austin 1975: Austin, John. *How to Do Things with Words*. Cambridge: Harvard University Press, 1975.

Avinery 1949: Avinery, Isaac. *Heical Rashi*. Tel-Aviv, 1949.

Ayer 1965: Ayer, A.J. *Philosophical Essays*. London: Macmillan & Co., Ltd., 1965.

Bahya 1980: R. Bahya ben Asher. *Encyclopedia of Torah Thoughts (Kad ha-Kemach)*. Translated by Charles B. Chavel. New York: Shilo Publishing House, 1980.

Barfield 1967: Barfield, Owen. *History in English Words*. London: Faber & Faber, 1953, Republished Grand Rapids: Eerdmans, 1967.

Barkay 1990: Barkay, Gabriel. "Bowl with Hebrew Inscription קדש." *IEJ* 40 (1990), 124-129.

Barton 2001: Barton, John. *Joel and Obadiah*. OTL. Louisville: Westminster John Knox Press, 2001.

Beentjes 1997. Beentjes, Pancratius. *The Book of Ben Sira in Hebrew*. Leiden/New York : Brill, 1997

Berkovits 2002: Berkovits, Eliezer. *Essential Essays on Judaism*. Jerusalem: Shalem Press, 2002.

Berman 1995: Berman, Joshua. *The Temple: Its Meaning and Symbolism Then and Now*. Northvale, NJ: Aronson, 1995.

Birnbaum 1977: Birnbaum, Philip. *Daily Prayer Book*. New York: Hebrew Publishing Company, 1977.

Bleich 1977: Bleich, J. David. *Contemporary Halakhic Problem: Volume I*. New York: KTAV, 1977.

Breuer 1988: Breuer, Joseph. *The Book of Jeremiah: Translation and Commentary*. Translated by Gertrude Hirschler. Spring Valley, NY: Feldheim Publishers, 1988.

Briggs 1906: Briggs Charles A. *A Critical and Exegetical Commentary on the Book of Psalms*, vol. 1. International Critical Commentary 14. New York: Scribner, 1906.

Burckhardt 1943: Burckhardt, Jacob. *Reflections on History*. Indianapolis: Liberty Fund, 1979, original 1943.

Cassuto 1987: Cassuto, Umberto. *A Commentary on the Book of Exodus*. Trans. Israel Abrahams. Jerusalem : Magnes Press, Hebrew University, 1987.

Cheyne 1884: Cheyne, Thomas Kelly. *The Book of Hosea*. Cambridge Bible for Schools and Colleges. Cambridge: Cambridge University Press, 1884.

Childs 1991: Childs, Brevard. *The Book of Exodus*. Old Testament Library. Philadelphia: Westminster, 1991.

Clines, n.d.: Clines, David J.A. "Alleged Basic Meanings of the Hebrew Verb qdš 'be holy': An Exercise in Comparative Hebrew Lexicography." Academia.edu

Cook 1974: Cook, Stanley Arthur. *A Glossary of the Aramaic Inscriptions.* Hildesheim ; New York : G. Olms, c1974.

Crenshaw 1995: Crenshaw, James L. *Joel.* AB. New York: Doubleday, 1995.

De Vaux 1961: De Vaux, Roland. *Ancient Israel: Its Life and Institutions.* Trans. John McHugh. New York: McGraw-Hill, 1961.

Del Olmo Lete 1999: Del Olmo Lete, Gregorio. *Canaanite Religion: According to the Liturgical Texts of Ugarit.* Trans. Wilfred G.E. Watson. Bethesda, MD: CDL Press, 1999.

Del Olmo Lete 2003: Del Olmo Lete & J. Sanmartín, *A Dictionary of the Ugaritic Language in the Alphabetic Tradition.* Trans. G.E. Watson. Boston: Brill, 2003.

Douglas 2002: Douglas, Mary. *Purity and Danger: An Analysis of Concept of Pollution and Taboo.* New York: Routledge Classics, 2002.

Durkheim 1915: Durkheim, Emile. *The Elementary Forms of the Religious Life.* Trans. Joseph Ward Swain. New York: The Free Press, 1915. Second printing 1965.

Eliade 1959: Eliade, Mircea. *The Sacred and the Profane: The Nature of Religion.* Translated by Willard R. Trask. New York: Harcourt, Inc., 1959.

Evans-Pritchard 1965: Evans-Pritchard, E.E. *Theories of Primitive Religion.* New York: Oxford University Press, 1965.

Feldman 1977: Feldman, Emanuel. *Biblical and Post-Biblical Defilement and Mourning: Law as Theology.* New York: Yeshiva University Press/KTAV Publishing House, 1977.

Feldman 1997: Feldman, Seymour. "Levi ben Gershom (Gersonides)." *History of Jewish Philosophy.* Edited by Daniel H. Frank and Oliver Leaman. London and New York: Routledge, 1997.

First 2015: First, Mitchell. *Esther Unmasked: Solving Eleven Mysteries of the Jewish Holidays and Liturgy.* New York: Kodesh Press, 2015.

Fitzmeyer and Harrington 1978: Fitzmeyer, Joseph A. and Daniel J. Harrington. *A Manual of Palestinian Aramaic Texts (Second Century B.C. – Second Century A.D.).* Rome: Biblical Institute Press, 1978.

Frankfort 1946: Frankfurt, Henri. *The Intellectual Adventure of Ancient Man.* Chicago, University of Chicago Press, 1946.

Frazer 1940: Frazer, James. *The Golden Bough.* New York: Macmillan, 1946.

Gammie 1989: Gammie, John. *Holiness in Israel.* Eugene, OR: Wipf and Stock Publishers, 1989.

Geller 1980: Geller, M.J. "The Šurpu Incantations and Lev. V. 1-5." *JSS* 25 (1980): 181-192.

Gibson 1982: Gibson, John C.L. *Textbook of Syrian Semitic Inscriptions: Volume III: Phoenician Inscriptions.* Oxford: Clarendon Press, 1982.

Gorman 1990: Gorman, Frank H., Jr. *Ideology of Ritual: Space, Time and Status in the Priestly Theology.* Journal for the Study of the Old Testament Supplement Series 91. Sheffield, England: JSOT Press, 1990.

Gray 1971: Gray, John. *I & II Kings: A Commentary.* Old Testament Library. Philadelphia: Westminster Press, 1971.

Greene 1929: Greene, Theodore Meyer, ed. *Kant Selections.* New York: Charles Scribner's Sons, 1929.

Harvey 1977: Harvey, Warren Zev. "Holiness: A Command to *Imitatio Dei.*" *Tradition* 16:3 (Spring 1977), 7-28.

Heschel 1965: Heschel, Abraham J. *Who is Man?* Stanford: Stanford University Press, 1965

Hildebrand 1989: Hildebrand, David. "Temple Ritual: A Paradigm for Moral Holiness in Haggai II 10-19." *VT* 39, Fasc. 2 (April 1989): 154-168.

Jacobus 1936: Jacobus, Melancthon, et al (eds.). *Funk and Wagnalls: A New Standard Bible Dictionary: Designed as a Comprehensive Help to the Study of the Scriptures, Their Languages, Literary Problems, History, Biography, Manners and Customs, and Their Religious Teachings.* New York: 1936, third edition.

James 1902: James, Williams. *The Varieties of Religious Experience.* New York: The Modern Library, 1902.

Jastrow 1903: Jastrow, Marcus. *Dictionary of the Targumum, Talmud Babli, Yerushalmi and Midrashic Literature.* Reprinted New York: Judaica Press, 1996.

Johnson 1979: Johnson, Samuel. *A Dictionary of the English Language.* Reprinted in facsimile. London: Times Books, 1979.

Jones 1984: *1 and 2 Kings*, vol. 2. New Century Bible Commentary. Grand Rapids: Eerdmans, 1984.

Kang 1989. Kang, Sa-Moon. *Divine War in the Old Testament and in the Ancient Near East.* Berlin/New York : W. de Gruyter, 1989.

Kaplan 1976: Kaplan, Aryeh. *Jerusalem: Eye of the Universe.* New York : National Conference of Synagogue Youth, 1976.

Kaplan 1991a: Kaplan, Aryeh. *The Aryeh Kaplan Anthology I: Maimonides' Principles; The Infinite Light; If You Were God; The Real Messiah?* New York, National Conference of Synagogue Youth, 1991.

Kaplan 1991b: Kaplan, Aryeh. *The Aryeh Kaplan Anthology II: Jerusalem; Sabbath; Tzitzith; Tefillin; Waters of Eden.* New York, National Conference of Synagogue Youth, 1991.

Kellner 2003: Kellner, Menachem. "Maimonides on the Nature of Ritual Purity and Impurity." *Daat: A Journal of Jewish Philosophy & Kabbalah* 50-52 (2003): I-XXX.

Kornfeld 1974: "קדש *qdš*." *Theological Dictionary of the Old Testament*, eds G. Johannes Botterweck and Helmer Ringgren, trans. John T. Willis. Grand Rapids: Eerdmans, 1977.

Krahmalkov 2000: Krahmalkov, Charles R. *Phoenician-Punic Dictionary.* Leuven: Uitgeverij Peeters en Dept. Oosterse Studies, 2000.

Lamm 1999: Lamm, Norman. *The Religious Thought of Hasidism.* Hoboken: KTAV, 1999.

Lasine 2010: Lasine, Stuart. "Everything Belongs to Me: Holiness, Danger, and Divine Kingship in the Post-Genesis World." *JSOT* 35:1 (2010): 31-62.

Leiser 1971: Leisier, Burton M. "The Sanctity of the Profane" A Phrasisaic Critique of Rudolf Otto." *Judaism* 20 (1971): 87-92.

Leslau 1987: Leslau, Wolf. *Comparative dictionary of Geʻez (Classical Ethiopic) : Geʻez-English, English-Geʻez, with an index of the Semitic roots.* Wiesbaden: O. Harrassowitz, 1987.

Levine 1989: Levine, Baruch. *Leviticus.* The JPS Torah Commentary. Philadelphia: The Jewish Publication Society, 1989.

Levine 1993: Levine, Baruch. *Numbers 1-20.* New York: Doubleday, 1993,

MacIntosh 1997: MacIntosh. A.A. *A Critical and Exegetical Commentary on Hosea.* ICC (new series). Edinburgh: T & T Clark, 1997.

Mauss 2000: Mauss, Marcel. *The Gift: The Form and Reason for Exchange in Archaic Societies*, trans. W.D. Halls. New York: W.W. Norton & Company, 2000.

Mays 1969: Mays, James Luther. *Hosea*. OTL. Philadelphia, The Westminster Press, 1969.

Meyers and Meyers 1998: Meyers, Carol L. and Eric M. Meyers. *Zechariah 9-14*. AB. New York: Doubleday, 1998.

Milgrom 1990: Milgrom, Jacob. *Numbers*. JPS. Philadelphia: The Jewish Publication Society Press, 1990.

Milgrom 1991: Milgrom, Jacob. *Leviticus 1-16*. The Anchor Bible. New York, Doubleday, 1991.

Milgrom 2000: Milgrom, Jacob. *Leviticus 17-22*. The Anchor Bible. New York: Doubleday, 2000.

Milgrom 2001: Milgrom, Jacob. *Leviticus 23-27*. The Anchor Bible. New York: Doubleday, 2001.

Muilenberg 1962: Muilenberg, J. "Holiness." *The Interpreter's Dictionary of the Bible: An Illustrated Encyclopedia*. 4 vols. Pages 616-625. New York, Abington Press, 1962.

Murtonen 1986-1990: Murtonen, A. *Hebrew in its West Semitic Setting*. New York: Brill, 1986-1990.

Novak, David. *The Theology of Nahmanides Theologically Presented*. 1992. Atlanta: Scholars Press, 1992.

Omanson 2008: Omanson, Roger L. and John E. Ellington. *A Handbook on 1-2 Kings*. New York: United Bible Societies, 2008.

Otto 1958: Otto, Rudolf. *The Idea of the Holy: An inquiry into the non-rational factor in the idea of the divine and its relation to the rational*. Translated by John W. Harvey. New York: Oxford University Press, 1958

Palmer 1976. Palmer, F.R. *Semantics*. New York: Cambridge University Press, 1976.

Pardee 2002: Pardee, Dennis. *Ritual and Cult at Ugarit.* Writings from the Ancient World 10. Atlanta: Society of Biblical Literature, 2002.

Paul 1991: Paul, Shalom. *Amos: A Commentary on the Book of Amos.* Minneapolis: Fortress Press, 1991.

Peli 1980: Peli, Pinchas H. *On Repentance in the Thought and Oral Discourses of Rabbi Joseph B. Soloveitchik.* Jerusalem: Oroth Publishing House, 1980.

Pentiuc 2001: Pentiuc, Eugen. *West Semitic Vocabulary in the Akkadian Texts from Emar.* Winona Lake, IN : Eisenbrauns, 2001.

Peterson 1984: Peterson, David L. *Haggah and Zechariah 1-8.* OTL. Philadelphia: The Westminster Press, 1984.

Propp 1999: Propp, William. *Exodus 1-18.* The Yale Anchor Bible Series. New York: Doubleday, 1999.

Propp 2006: Propp, William H.C. *Exodus 19-40.* The Yale Anchor Bible Series. New York: Doubleday, 2006.

Reif 1972: Reif, S.C. "Dedicated to חנך." *VT* 22 (1972): 495-501.

Roth 1974: Roth, Sol. *"Sanctity and Separation." Tradition* 14:4 (1974).

Rynhold 2009: Rynhold, Daniel. *An Introduction to Medieval Jewish Philosophy.* New York: I.B. Taurus, 2009.

Sarna 1966: Sarna, Nahum. *Understanding Genesis.* New York: Jewish Theological Seminary of America, 1966.

Sarna 1986: Sarna, Nahum. *Exploring Exodus.* New York: Schocken, 1986.

Sarna 1989: Sarna, Nahum. *Exodus.* JPS. Philadelphia: The Jewish Publication Society Press, 1989.

Sarna 1993: Sarna, Nahum. *On the Book of Psalms.* New York: Schocken, 1993.

Schachter 2010: Schachter, Herschel. *Divrei HaRav: Maran Yosef Dov HaLevi Soloveitchik, z.tz.l* (Hebrew). New York: OU Press 2010.

Schlick, Moritz. "What is the Aim of Ethics?" *Logical Positivism,* ed. A.J. Ayer. Glencoe, Illinois: The Free Press, 1959

Segal 1989: Segal, Peretz. "The Divine Verdict of Leviticus X 3." *VT* 39:1 (1989), 91-95.

Shamah 2011: Shamah, Moshe. *Recalling the Covenant.* Jersey City, NJ: KTAV, 2011.

Shapiro 1964: Shapiro, David. "The Meaning of Holiness in Judaism." *Tradition* 7:1 (1964), pp. 46-80.

Smith 1889: Smith, W. Robertson. *The Religion of the Semites.*

Snaith 1964: Snaith, Norman H. *The Distinctive Ideas of the Old Testament.* New York: Schocken Books, 1964.

Soloveitchik 1983: Soloveitchik, J.B. *Halakhic Man.* Translated by Lawrence Kaplan. Philadelphia: The Jewish Publication Society, 1983.

Soloveitchik 2003: Soloveitchik, J.B. *Worship of the Heart.* Ed. Shalom Carmy. New York: KTAV, 2003.

Soloveitchik 2005a: Soloveitchik, J.B. *Community, Covenant and Commitment: Selected Letters and Communications.* MeOztar HoRav 4. Ed. Nathaniel Helfgot. New York: KTAV, 2005.

Soloveitchik 2005b: Soloveitchik, J.B. *The Emergence of Ethical Man.* MeOztar HoRav 5. Ed. Michael S. Berger. New York: KTAV, 2005.

Soloveitchik 2008: Soloveitchik, J.B. *And From There You Shall Seek.* Trans. Naomi Goldblum. New York: KTAV, 2008.

Steiner 1998: Steiner, Richard C. "Saadia vs. Rashi: On the Shift from Meaning-Maximalism to Meaning-Minimalism in Medieval Biblical Lexicology." *JQR* NS 88: 3/4 (Jan.-Apr. 1998): 213-258.

Streetman 1980: Streetman, Robert F. "Some Later Thoughts of Otto on the Holy." *Journal of the American Academy of Religion*, 48:3 (Sept. 1980), 365-384.

Student 2018. Student, Gil. *Search Engine: Finding Meaning in Jewish Texts: Volume 2: Jewish Leadership*. New York: Kodesh Press, 2018.

Sullivan 1989: Sullivan, Roger J. *Immanuel Kant's Moral Theory*. New York: Cambridge University Press, 1989. Reprinted 1990, 1991, 1995.

Tawil 2009: Tawil, Hayim. *An Akkadian Lexical Companion of Biblical Hebrew*. Jersey City: KTAV Publishing House, 2009.

Tawil 2012: Tawil, Hayim. *Lexical Studies in the Bible and Ancient Near Eastern Inscriptions: The Collected Essays of Hayim Tawil*. Eds. Abraham Jacob Berkovitz, Stuart W. Halpern and Alec Goldstein. New York: Yeshiva University Press, 2012.

Tillich 1955: Tillich, Paul. *Biblical Religion and the Search for Ultimate Reality*. Chicago: University of Chicago Press, 1955.

Tomback 1978: Tomback, Richard. *A Comparative Semitic Lexicon of the Phoenician and Punic Languages*. Missoula, Montana: Scholars Press, 1978.

Twersky 1980: Twersky, Isadore. *Introduction to the Code of Maimonides* (Mishneh Torah). Yale Judaica Series XXII. New Haven: Yale University Press, 1980.

Van der Toorn 1985: Van der Toorn, K. *Sin and Sanction in Israel and Mesopotamia: A Comparative Study*. Studia Semitica Neerlandica. Assen/Maastricht, The Netherlands: Van Gorcum, 1985.

Van Inwagen 2009: Van Inwagen, Peter. *Metaphysics*. Boulder, CO.: Westview, 2009.

Van Koppen 1999: Van Koppen, F. and K. Van der Toorn. "Holy One." *Dictionary of Deities and Demons in the Bible*, 415-418. Edited by Karel van der Toorn et al. Boston: Brill, 1999.

Wakefield 1987: Wakefield, Jerome. "Why Justice and Holiness Are Similar: 'Protagoras' 330-331." *Phronesis* 32:3 (1987): 267-276.

Whitehead 1926: Whitehead, Alfred North. *Religion in the Making*. New York: Meridian Books, 1926, reprinted 1960.

Williamson 2008: Williamson, H.G.M. *Holy, Holy, Holy: The Story of a Liturgical Formula*. Berlin: De Gruyter, 2008.

Wilson 1994: Wilson, E. Jan. *"Holiness" and "Purity" in Mesopotamia*. Neukirchener Verlag, 1994.

Wittgenstein 1965: Wittgenstein, Ludwig. "A Lecture on Ethics," *The Philosophical Review*, 74:1 (Jan. 1965): 3-12.

Wright 1992: Wright, David P. "Holiness (OT)." *Anchor Bible Dictionary*, ed. D.N. Freedman. New York: Doubleday, 1992.

Zafrani 2005: Zafrani, Haim. *Two Thousand Years of Jewish Life in Morocco*. New York: Sephardic House, 2005.

Zimmels 1997: Zimmels, H.J. *Ashkenazim and Sephardim: Their Relations, Differences, and Problems as Reflected in the Rabbinical Responsa (Revised Edition)*. Library of Sephardic History and Thought. New York: KTAV, 1997.

38131127R00157

Made in the USA
Columbia, SC
06 December 2018